SEA WATER AQUARIA

SEA WATER AQUARIA

L. A. J. JACKMAN, FZS
Member of the Marine Biological Association UK

SOUTH BRUNSWICK AND NEW YORK
A. S. BARNES AND COMPANY

First American edition published 1975
A. S. Barnes and Company Inc.,
Cranbury, New Jersey 08512

Library of Congress Catalog Card Number: 74-11588
ISBN 0-498-01649-8

Printed in Great Britain

CONTENTS

CONTENTS

6

LIST OF ILLUSTRATIONS

PLATES

All photographs not otherwise acknowledged are from the author's collection.

7

FIGURES

PREFACE

Wherever you may live, in a city or within reach of salt spray, a successful marine aquarium can be yours. The sea offers a host of fascinating creatures, whose strange and beautiful shapes and intriguing habits, can be watched within the smallest aquarium tank. This book shows you how to be successful and explains how easy these creatures are to keep.

No other aquarist can experience the vast range of life that is available to the marine enthusiast. Fish of diverse shape and colour, crabs in endless variety, beautiful anemones, starfish and urchins, worms, sea squirts and a host of others can be kept in fish-house or sitting-room. At home for your pleasure, or in school as an educational resource, marine life will provide an absorbing interest, and for the naturalist, a new field of discovery.

Our hobby grows apace and the coming years will see marine aquaria develop into a major interest among all those countless folk who delight in living animals.

This book replaces my earlier volume, *Marine Aquaria*, and incorporates a great deal of new information learnt by continued experience and demanded by a rich variety of new equipment reinforced by new practices.

No longer is a marine aquarium the realm of the specialist.

1

THE SEA

CYCLE OF LIFE IN THE SEA

The fertility of the sea can be compared quite closely with that of the average acre of farmland, and the major portion of this fertility is derived from the countless millions of microscopic plants and animals that live their brief life beneath the sunlit surface of the seas.

If only we could submerge and evolve eyes that could magnify like the lens of a microscope, the variety of life before us would defy description. Within a few seconds of our first glimpse we should see enacted a thousand deaths and a thousand births, for in these pastures of the sea the struggle for survival is as continuous as the tides that carry this drifting population, the plankton.

Plankton, in the economy of the sea, is the vital thread that floats on all the tides. Yet without the sunlight and the ceaseless rhythm of the seasons, the sea might become as barren as a gaunt cliff face. The cycle of life in the sea goes something like this . . .

In the spring as the sun mounts higher in the sky the light becomes more intense and the one-celled plants begin to thrive. However, they need more than sunlight, and draw on a great store of minerals that has been slowly built up during the winter days and nights. These minerals are the 'salts' of the sea and are the equivalent of the natural fertilisers found in the rotting vegetation on land. They come from the decaying bodies of countless sea life. Since during the winter months there has been a constant accumulation of these salts, the sea is much richer in early spring, pasture for the growth that is fostered by the sunlight. So the plankton increase suddenly. Countless millions of phyto-plankton (plants) swarm in the surface waters as the fish, crabs, and shellfish prepare to bear their young, for fundamentally the animals depend upon the plants for their first food.

Finally, prompted by temperature, light, and other factors, the peak period of spawning is reached. What this means in terms of numbers can best be gauged by thinking about the numbers of eggs deposited by sea fish. Firstly, species that deposit their eggs on rock surfaces seldom lay more than a thousand. Secondly (and here comes the challenge to survival), species that lay floating eggs release their eggs in millions. The turbot, for instance, releases about eight million eggs, and the great floating egg-ribbons of the angler fish may contain twenty or more millions. Multiply these figures by the number of mature fish spawning each spring, and you have some idea of the terrific increase of life that occurs at this time of year.

The millions of eggs that were never fertilised fall to the bottom, and on the sea bed decay and release their microcosm of mineral salts as a contribution to the food supply of more fortunate brethren. In time, frequently only a few days, these latter hatch from the egg, equipped with a yolk-sac as their first food. In the space of little more than a week, the yolk-sacs have been absorbed and the post-larval fish begin to feed on the drifting plankton. Their stomachs become filled with the tiny plants and growth is rapid. But a very sudden decline in the numbers of plants occurs in consequence.

Thus by the end of the spring the plant plankton reaches its lower limit, and of the eight million eggs of our turbot, fewer than two dozen remain as living fry. The rest have provided food for the larval crabs, young jellyfish and other predators.

The seasonal cycle passes into summer. Now the surface waters warm up and 'layering' occurs, as a kind of thermal barrier is built up a few fathoms down from the surface. Beneath this barrier, the mineral salts are trapped, and whilst there is sufficient sunlight for growth of plant plankton, there is little food in the form of minerals, for this has already been depleted in the upper waters during the spring.

With the coming of autumn, the first gales churn up the waters, the barrier is broken down, and the mineral salts mix in with the surface waters. As there is plenty of sunlight left, a fresh increase of plankton occurs. This, however, is short-lived. And so comes the winter.

Unfortunately we cannot reproduce these conditions in an aquarium, although there are similarities in a small way, a very small way. For instance, during early spring, February and March in the northern hemisphere, if you keep hermit crabs you will be able to watch them release their young, but unless a constant supply of sea water is available you will not succeed in rearing them. In the clear filtered water of the home aquarium the seasons pass unnoticed and only behaviour can be observed, unless the aquarist is prepared to haul vast quantities of sea water home, having a circulating system fixed up, or go to work with a plankton tow net.

That cautionary word should not deter the keen aquarist, for as indicated in another section of the book, it can be, and indeed it HAS been done.

CHEMICAL PROPERTIES OF SEA WATER

COMPOSITION. Reference has already been made to the minerals released by decaying animal life within the sea, and for a moment it might be as well to take a look at the actual chemicals which together 'make the sea salt'.

A short walk along the tide-line when the surf is rolling shorewards soon brings the tang of salt to the lips, and the white ruination of sea-soaked leather shoes is an indication of the quantity of this salt in even a small amount of sea water. If you take a bucketful of sea water and evaporate it, a white crystalline substance remains. On an average, the quantity of salts is about 35 parts to 1,000 parts of water by weight. Near a river estuary it will be considerably less, and in the Red Sea, for instance, considerably more. Even in the Red Sea, however, it is only around 40 parts to 1,000.

The salt in our bucket is about 75 per cent sodium chloride. If the bucket held two gallons of water, there would be about half a pound. The remainder of the salts would comprise sulphates, bromides, and carbonates of sodium, potassium, calcium, and magnesium, plus minute traces of other elements.

Because sea water is such a delicate balance of minerals, many a keen aquarist has encountered difficulties. Many of the salts react with certain metals such as brass, galvanised iron, copper, and even lead to an extent sufficient to produce a solution poisonous to fish and other living creatures in your aquarium. Thus it is essential for the marine aquarium keeper to take great care in his choice of materials and equipment.

ARTIFICIAL SEA WATER. Whilst on the topic of sea-water chemistry, it may be as well to include a formula for those who wish to make their own. The following formula was given me by Mr F. A. J. Armstrong of the Plymouth Marine Biological Laboratory and is one which has been used quite successfully for the rearing of Echinus larvae.

$NaCl$	23·477g	$NaHCO_3$	0·192
$MgCl_2$	4·981	KBr	0·096
Na_2SO_4	3·917	H_3BO_3	0·026
$CaCl_2$	1·102	$SrCl_2$	0·024
KCl	0·664	NaF	0·003

Water to 1,000 grams. Aerate before use

This yields sea water, salinity 34·5, pH between 7·9 and 8·3. The accuracy with which some of the weights are given is probably needlessly great for normal work.

Water of crystallisation in some of the salts must be allowed for, and the $MgCl_2$ and $CaCl_2$ are possible to weigh since they are hygroscopic and contain unknown amounts of water. Solutions can be made up and standardised, and you can take the volume necessary to give the correct weight. Trace elements are difficult, but by using analytical reagent chemicals one can keep them fairly low. Mr Armstrong mentions the fact that he keeps a set of reagents aside for artificial sea water in order to ensure that batches made at different times are constant in this respect.

It can be seen that the making of such artificial sea water is not an easy task and that great accuracy has to be aimed at. But any local pharmacist will make up the desired quantities if you present him with this formula.

SEA TEMPERATURE

Around the shallow water of our coasts there is a great seasonal variation in temperatures. In winter it may go as low as freezing point, whilst during a hot summer the figure of 66° F may well be attained. This great temperature variation causes movements of fish and other creatures in and out between deeper water and shallow water. For instance, the movement of mackerel is perhaps as well known as any. Now these fish first appear inshore soon after the sea reaches 53° F and they remain until the temperature returns to about that level. More accurate figures are shown in a paper mentioned at the end of this book.

Although this wide temperature variation occurs, it must not be imagined that the creatures of the shore will tolerate sudden changes in your aquarium. Always remember that most of the actively swimming ones will be well offshore before the cold weather sets in. In your aquarium they are trapped, so keep that temperature steady.

It is impossible in the limited space of a single chapter to give details of the temperature preferences of each species. However, it is safe to say that most of the commoner seashore species are quite hardy and can endure variation better than their deep-water counterparts. Frequently during the summer months, anemones that have been brought in from deep water will close up and refuse to open when introduced into tanks that are warmer.

LIGHT IN THE SEA

In the seas the light intensity varies according to depth. As the depth increases so the amount of light decreases until final and absolute darkness prevails. The aquarist is not likely to meet an animal from such depths, and even if he did he would find it impossible to keep alive because of the high pressure required.

In addition to the decrease of light according to depth, there is the daily cycle of light and dark, seasonal variations and the day to day differences according to weather conditions.

From observational work at sea, it is obvious that the vast majority of sea creatures shun the intense sunlight, and this has a profound effect on the movement of fish, especially in so far as swimming depth is concerned. On bright summer days fish go deep during the hours of midday, but at dawn they will be found up on the surface. At night, as soon as dusk has fallen, the fish tend to rise towards the surface. This behaviour is often due to the movements of their prey, who are sometimes more sensitive still to light intensity.

Thus in the seas there is a natural movement of certain species away from intense light, and this can be seen quite plainly when fish are first introduced into a brightly lit tank. They will strive to find shade, and if this is not available, will rush madly about, both damaging themselves and spreading panic to the rest of the fish.

Newly caught fish should be placed in a semi-darkened tank. This is most easily effected by covering it with a sheet of paper or cloth, and this should be left for five or six hours before moving it slightly to admit first a glimmer and later diffuse light. After some ten hours the cover can be completely removed. Even then new fish will continue to hide away during daylight hours for as long as a week, probably coming out only at night.

In this short chapter a few ideas have been included to show the general effect of certain conditions within the waters on the fish that live there. The true picture is very complex, and biologists today are much concerned with the effect of temperature and light and various other factors, but a great bulk of knowledge has already been written up. Aquarists will find much useful information in the reference books mentioned at the end of this book.

The aquarist wishing to obtain the very best out of his marine aquarium would be wise to learn as much as possible about conditions in the sea, for in that way he will gain a deeper understanding of the requirements of his charges.

Fundamentally, life in the sea is very closely knit. The sea gives all, and in return demands all. In the process of this cycle a bountiful harvest is inevitable.

2

THE CONSTRUCTION OF MARINE AQUARIUM TANKS

As already discussed in Chapter 1, sea water has highly corrosive properties, and thus the choice of material for tank construction is rather limited unless very careful proofing of the exposed parts is carried out. If we assume that correct proofing can be given, we are still faced with the problem of tank size, for any aquarist making his own tanks will have to consider the matters of weight and cost.

As an example let us take what will probably be the largest size attempted by any amateur, and presume its measurements to be 4ft long by 2ft wide and 2ft in depth. If it is to be built of angle-iron, the sheets of plate glass will be both expensive and heavy, and by the time the tank is filled you will be getting near three-quarters of a ton total weight. You will also have glass all around, and since this does not lend itself to the best presentation of marine life you will probably decide to paint over the back and ends, in some form of 'black out'.

Why go to such trouble and use such unsuitable materials when wood makes a far better and more efficient tank? However, for those of you who really do prefer all-glass tanks, fuller details follow later in this chapter.

Wood has certain clear-cut advantages for tank construction:

a) It is easily worked and a good finish can be expected.
b) It is light and durable.
c) It is a fairly good insulator and will help to preserve a steady temperature.

d) If through faulty workmanship repairs become necessary, then the job is quite simple.

e) Airlines, filters, etc, can easily be attached to the woodwork.

f) It is absolutely non-contaminating.

The disadvantages of wood must also be mentioned, although they are far outweighed by the advantages.

a) It tends to warp and shrink if it is not properly seasoned.

b) Marine wood-boring creatures such as the gribble will sometimes make an attack on the framework.

METHOD OF CONSTRUCTION

The secret of making leak-proof marine aquaria in wood lies in the use of marine glues. For those not acquainted with these glues it should be explained that they can be purchased in packets containing a powdered resin-based material which is mixed with cold water and a transparent hardening fluid. The glue (resin-base) is applied to one of the surfaces, whilst the hardener is applied to the other. When these two surfaces are brought together a chemical reaction takes place and a perfect watertight joint results. Full instructions are contained in the packs.

With these glues you cannot go wrong, and the next matter to be decided is a choice of wood. In the past teak has always been recommended, but today it is very expensive. We have used parana pine with great success and the chart below shows suggested thicknesses for various sizes of tank.

	THICKNESS OF WOOD	
LENGTH OF TANK	BASE	SIDES
Up to 2′	1″	$\frac{3}{4}$″ to 1″
2′ to 3′	1″	1″
3′ to 4′	$1\frac{1}{2}$″	$1\frac{1}{2}$″

Parana pine is easily worked, but when ordering it make sure it is free from 'shakes' or cracks, for although the marine glue will seal them they are frequently a source of trouble in the future. Watch out for minute worm-holes that seem to appear in some pieces; however, these are not a serious problem for they can be plugged and sealed—although once again it is best to get a perfect sample of timber by persevering.

When bought straight from the timber yard, parana pine is often unseasoned, and if you store it for any length of time you will probably find it is well and truly warped when you come to use it. Thus, never buy your timber until you are ready to start on the actual construction of the tank.

The matter of correct jointing is one in which craftsmen will have preconceived opinions based on experience with wood, but an ordinary butt joint (Fig 1) will make a perfectly strong and waterproof joint and will be durable.

As an illustration of this kind of joint we once made one with marine glue, and then after it had set tried to break it down. One piece was put into a vice and the other hit with a wooden mallet low down on the actual joint. It did not budge and further pulling with two hands eventually broke the wood itself, leaving the joint intact! After all, if you have this kind of strength in a glue why complicate things by extravagant jointing?

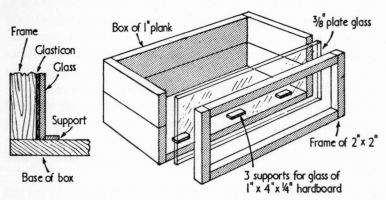

Seal glass to frame with layer of Glasticon ¼" thick when in position. Join component parts of tank together with marine glue; screws should not be necessary

Fig 1 Construction of aquarium tank

In Fig 1 the illustrations show you how to make a wooden tank and little further explanation is necessary.

Having made the tank it must be proofed with a reliable and non-contaminating bituminous paint, such as Bituros. These paints are obtainable in black and colours, and although few believe it at first hearing, the black is ideal as a background for marine animals.

Marine ply has much to commend it. It can be purchased in large sheets of varying thickness, a useful sheet size being 8ft by 4ft. It is tough, durable and exceedingly waterproof—even after prolonged immersion. It does tend to be rather more expensive than parana pine, but can be used as a base in combination with parana pine for the sides. We have one tank 6ft long by 4ft wide and 3ft deep in which the base is ½in thick marine ply and the sides 1in thick parana pine, joined along their edges with marine glue until the desired width is reached.

Remember it must be marine ply, *not* just any plywood or you will soon get trouble.

OTHER MATERIALS

METAL CONTAINERS. Under this category comes a wide range of metals, some of which must be regarded with care. Of the dangerous ones, galvanised iron is first. An old cistern, providing it is not too rusted, can soon be made into a useful tank—but you must make quite sure it is well protected with a bituminous paint, which must be applied to a perfectly rust-free surface. That's not as easy as it sounds, for it means several hours of tedious cleaning with emery paper and files and scraping with wire brushes, for if the rust is left and then covered with paint within a month you will have the paint lifting—and trouble starting.

All that needs to be done with this sort of tank is to cut out your front window with a hacksaw and providing a 2in margin is left all around the outside edge you can make your window any shape or size you choose. Porthole tanks can be made in this way.

Tin is another metal that can be used successfully in the construction of small aquaria and is ideal for small seashells or other small creatures. These tanks are easily made, but first of all run some solder down the joints at the sides and around the bottom to make sure they are leak-proof. Tins are usually jointed by a folding of the corners and these never hold water for any length of time. The window can be cut out with wire-cutters or an old pair of scissors.

Since the edge so cut is seldom a good glazing surface, the glazing medium must be applied a little thicker than usual. Paint with bituminous paint and fill with fresh tap water for a week before use, making sure you have the tank resting where you intend to keep it. It may leak a little from the glazing at first, but this will soon stop. Never move these tanks or fresh leaks will start.

So much for tins then. They make good small tanks, but must be treated with extra care. If a number of these are used in a line they can be most effective in displaying a selection of one species. But beware of all aluminium ware. It was never intended for marine aquarium work, and will soon convince you of the fact.

CONCRETE. Waterproof cements can be used in the making of frames, but they are rather heavy and unwieldy, and probably not of great use to home aquarists. Unless very well made by someone used to working in this medium, leaks will occur, both from joints and from the cement surface itself. Reinforcing must be done skilfully or else rust will work itself out through the cement.

Concrete as a material for the construction of large tanks in commercial aquaria is, however, becoming increasingly popular.

GLASS BATTERY JARS. Still obtainable from some pet shops are the glass battery cases once used in power stations. Whilst these make fairly good containers the glass is of poor quality. The consequent distortion makes such a case a bad buy for any aquarist who wishes to display good specimens.

As a container for live foods, however, they are ideal.

MOULDED ALL-GLASS TANKS. All good stockists have these tanks, and they are perfectly good, and of course are free from any contaminating material, being of glass only. The one great disadvantage is that three sides need to be blacked-out to get the best effect.

All glass tanks are quite easy to make, but unless you are an expert glass-cutter, do have the glass cut to size professionally.

Sides and bottom are stuck together edge to edge with one of the proprietary brands of silicone adhesive sold in pet shops, hardware and do-it-yourself stores.

The base too can be glass, but this needs to be a little thicker than the sides. For tanks up to 15in by 9in use 32oz glass for the base, and 24oz for the sides (32oz if you prefer an extra safety margin).

A simple wood framework can be made to hold the sides together until the silicone sets, but in very small tanks the adhesive will be sufficiently tacky to hold your tank together right from the start.

PLASTIC TANKS. Many different forms of plastic have been adapted to aquarium use and all are completely non-contaminating. Polystyrene tanks are cheap, but due to the somewhat brittle nature of the plastic it is unwise to move the tank when filled. Some of these designs incorporate simple covers with strip lights.

Any aquarist wishing to keep a maximum number of species in separate tanks at a low cost can do so with these.

A new process combines the strength of iron without its rusting. The tank frame is simply dip-coated with polythene and in general it is thick enough to resist minor scratching.

STAINLESS STEEL. With the development of new methods of construction, stainless-steel aquaria are no longer the expense they once were. Small light-gauge stainless-steel tanks are easy to use and of pleasing appearance and any excess salt caused by evaporation on the surface of the metal is easily wiped away with a damp cloth. There are, of course, no rust problems.

PLASTIC CONTAINERS. Every hardware store today has a display of clear plastic containers used as food covers, tea and sugar containers and so on. Many of these can be used as rearing tanks for small fish and brine shrimps, and also for keeping solitary small species for short periods of time. As I write I am using two plastic sandwich boxes to rear a few dozen baby pipefish and in such a limited space the food is kept near them and their growth is all the faster in consequence. Beside these is a battery of shallow containers in which a series of brine shrimps are being reared as food. Every three days a new batch of eggs is hatched and in this way a continuous food supply is ensured.

POOLS. Plastic pools as sold for garden use make excellent 'rock pools'. A small one can be fitted into a wooden framework and used as a table tank. With careful display and use of rocks it can be turned into a good replica. Many of these pools measure about 4ft by 3ft by 12in deep and are of irregular shape with a natural rock finish.

The top edge is normally bent at right angles to form a flat rim 1in wide and this can be screwed into the wooden supporting framework where it makes contact. The usual filtration systems can be applied, but artificial lighting is best applied from the front by using a strip lamp in a low cover.

Improvised and temporary pools can be easily constructed, using a sheet of polythene spread around the inside of a wooden or cardboard box. Heavy-gauge polythene should be used and a band of string or wire around the outside of the box makes the whole thing stronger.

PLASTIC BUCKETS AND DUSTBINS. The plastic buckets most useful to the marine aquarist are those of rectangular shape: these are stable when used for collecting, and make good reservoirs and store tanks. Large and small dustbins are useful as larger-capacity reservoirs and for transporting larger specimens by car.

ANGLE-IRON TANKS. As mentioned earlier in the chapter, these can be adapted for marine use. To do this proof all joints and surfaces with several coats of Bituros to prevent rusting and make quite sure the material used in the angles is iron and not any alloy metal likely to harm the fish. In the joints between the glasses down the sides there is often a space, admittedly small, where sea water can attack the metal. To prevent damage here, run a layer of Glasticon into the joint by pressing it into place with the finger.

OTHER TYPES OF AQUARIA

By their very nature many marine animals are admirably suited to life in a pond, and such ponds can be constructed in a number of ways.

The first and most obvious, perhaps, is to use an old sink. Providing it is not cracked, the outflow should be sealed up with a cork or wood bung and made waterproof with a layer of glazing compound. As a means of keeping live foods such as prawn, this form of tank is ideal, but if you wish to make it more natural then it is simplicity itself to arrange rockwork by cementing all around the sides. If such rockwork is allowed to come above the level of the edge of your sink, it can be made to resemble some rock pool in perfect detail.

Most sinks have an overflow outlet at the top, above the drainaway. If this is left uncovered, crabs and prawns will be continually crawling down the vent and dying, so fill it in with concrete or cement. This will also prevent water dripping down and tending to smell.

One most effective table-tank I know is made from wood lined with asphalt. Such tanks can be made to any size you choose, and although the water must necessarily be shallow, it will prove ideal for many seashore creatures. The one great drawback with these tanks is that friends are too liable to want to touch everything.

In the making of this form of tank, good thick wood should be used, and a firm base in the form of a table is essential, otherwise warping will start leaks. Butt-jointed, and sealed with marine glue, your table-tank will last for years and be perfectly trouble-free providing you have it well aerated, and do not overcrowd with specimens.

GLAZING THE TANK

Glazing is one of those jobs where an ounce of practical experience is worth a ton of theory, but for beginners the following pitfalls are listed and ways of overcoming them mentioned.

Firstly, it matters little of what material the tank is made, for the first principle of getting a sound leak-proof joint applies to most materials the aquarist is likely to use.

There are innumerable glazing compounds on the market, and some of them are excellent. When choosing material the following requirements should be borne in mind:

a) The compound should be easily worked.
b) It should be sufficiently firm to remain in place after application with a knife.
c) It must be completely free from all lumps and hard pieces.
d) It must remain soft and pliable throughout the life of the tank. Glazing compounds that go hard merely start leaks and are a source of never-ending trouble.

Now to presume your 2ft tank is ready for glazing. First thoroughly clean all surfaces of the glass and make perfectly sure that the edges in particular are clean and free from grease, dampness and dirt. Next, make sure the surfaces of the bearing members are clean, whether these are angle-iron, wood, or concrete. Such surfaces must also be smooth.

Take a small quantity of the glazing compound and work it about as for putty until it is fairly pliable. Take a piece about the size of a plum in your hand and roll it out between your fingers until a long string about ⅜in in diameter is produced. Place this string on the aquarium surface that is to be glazed. Press lightly into place so that it will remain there until you are prepared to put the glass in position.

Having pressed the compound all the way round the surface, next place the glass inside the aquarium. Press it lightly at first on to the compound and then increase the pressure until the compound begins to squeeze out all the way round. Keep pressing until the glass has about an ⅛in compound between it and the tank. The tank is now ready for filling.

If leaks occur when filling it is a simple job to press a little extra compound from the outside into the area where the water is seeping out. As soon as the water pressure increases as you fill the tank, all leaks will stop.

It may seem strange advice, to say that the compound should be rolled into a 'string', and not applied flatly and neatly with a glazing tool. The reason is simply that the smaller surface area of the 'string' allows the glass to be pressed more easily into place and the consequent flattening of the compound will give the same result. If you spread the glazing compound as a flat surface, it is surprising how difficult it is to press the glass home and thus make a watertight joint.

If the tank to be glazed is a large one, say 4ft long, then a different method can be employed. Preparation of surfaces is just as important, but the 'roll' of glazing compound should be of at least $\frac{3}{4}$in diameter. It will be appreciated that a sheet of $\frac{3}{8}$in plate glass 4ft by 2ft will be very heavy to handle, and unless care is taken it is all too easy to cut your hands. Use a piece of cloth to grip the glass and make sure your hands are free from grease.

However, before introducing the glass into the tank you should have four or five lengths of wood and a couple of wedges ready. These pieces of wood will be used to force the glass into place and need to be slightly longer than the width of the tank.

Next place three strips of $\frac{1}{4}$in wood about 2in wide by 1ft long on the floor of the tank against the bottom glazing bar. These will keep the bottom surface of the glass clear of the tank base, and make it much easier to push it into place, as it reduces the friction that would result if the entire length of the glass were resting on the tank base.

The glass can now be lifted into place inside the tank and lowered on to the three thin strips.

Next, place one piece of wood at each corner and one in the middle of your glass, with their other ends resting lightly against the back of the tank. Now, by judicious placing of wedges between the ends of the wood and the back of the tank you can exert pressure on the glass. Do this gradually and evenly until the glass is well bedded.

As the tank is filled the pressure increases and pieces of wood will float free and can be removed.

The golden rules for a watertight glazing joint are simple:

careful preparation of the surfaces, steady pressure when applying the glass to the joint and—most important of all—the use of a reliable, non-drying glazing medium.

TEMPORARY GLAZING. Here is a simple method of glazing a tank to be used for certain limited purposes, like being taken to the shore when specimens are to be photographed. Place a length of thin rubber tubing all around the joint surface where the glass is to fit. Press the glass home against this soft rubber and keep it in place by means of a few lengths of wood wedged against the glass. Fill the tank and, always providing the frame is true, it will be perfectly watertight.

Such simplicity sounds impossible, yet on one occasion we glazed a tank with rubber draught-excluder in order to discover if it would remain watertight for any length of time. The tank was 4ft long by 2ft deep. That tank did not leak a drop as it was filled and remained perfectly watertight for a year. It was still holding water when we decided the experiment had continued long enough.

For tanks likely to be moved a great deal, rubber compound can be used successfully, but it must be emphasised that this is not easy to apply. As a glazing medium for tin tanks it is quite successful, as it grips the smooth but rippled surface with great tenacity. Used with these tins it gives a certain rigidity to the tank that could never be obtained with ordinary semi-plastic glazing mediums.

Last, but by no means least, never use putty. Putty is made for glazing windows, not aquarium tanks.

3

PREPARATION OF THE TANKS

ROCKWORK

There is no doubt that rockwork can make or mar your aquarium, and it is well worth while spending time arranging the rocks in different ways before deciding on their final position. By asking yourself three questions you will find the job is simplified considerably.

1. What am I going to keep? Make a list of the specimens you intend to keep in the particular tank under consideration, and then ask yourself question 2.

2. What particular consideration must I give to their special requirements? For instance, your list may consist of shore crabs, hermit crabs, mussels, anemones and prawns.

From this list you can see that the anemones can be quite at home on rock ledges, and a small cave can be provided for the shore crabs. A few ledges or overhanging rocks will provide a stamping ground for the hermits, and perhaps a sloping rock could be provided for the mussels. If fish had been included in the list you might have added a small rock pinnacle for wrasse, or a seashell for a two-spot goby, and so on.

You may feel that all this thinking beforehand is a waste of time, and that the aquarium is seldom made that will contain one set community for any length of time. But it is surprising how attached the aquarist becomes to certain creatures and few of us are prepared to return well-known animals to the shore. The time will surely come when you also want new creatures, and that is the moment to build or buy the next tank. So set up this one with some definite plan in mind.

The third and last question is one that must inevitably be answered by compromise.

3. How can I place the rocks so that maximum visibility is attained? A cave, for instance, can be a compromise between the darkness of a submarine cleft and the half-light of a shore-line cave. The roof part can slope sharply backwards to allow light to penetrate or a piece of glass can be set in the top.

Having decided on the general layout of the rocks, the next decision is on the type of stone to use. A natural effect can be attained only by using natural rocks and assembling them in their own particular stratified way. Unless you bear this fact in mind your rockwork will resemble a pile of untidy and uninteresting stones that constantly offend the eye. Fig 2 give typical rock arrangements.

If possible keep to one kind of rock, and do not try to mix red sandstone in with limestone as a background. Rocks can be mixed fairly effectively on the bed of the aquarium, but the restricted vista of the tank back is far too small to allow this to be done.

Having secured sufficient rocks for your purpose (and it is always a good plan to have far more than you think you will require), wash them thoroughly in fresh tap water to remove all salt. Next scrub them with a wire brush to remove seaweed growth, dirt and adhering shellfish. The weed will only die whilst the aquarium is seasoning, the dirt prevents the cement getting a good grip, and the shellfish are not required yet anyway. Leave the now clean rocks in a basin of water to soak thoroughly, before cementing into place. Ordinary cement can be used but it does break down due to reaction with sea water and it is safer to use the special brands made for use in sea water. Aquacrete is excellent.

SETTING THE ROCKS IN PLACE. Since loose rocks invite trouble and also provide hiding-places, rockwork should be fixed permanently in place with cement. In this way all cracks can be effectively sealed and many troubles prevented.

Fig 2 Suggested placing of rocks etc in an aquarium

Providing the aquarium can be left for about two or three weeks to 'season', ordinary cement is quite satisfactory. It causes a few disturbing features to develop, however, in the first few days after filling. Usually you will find a few stalagmite-like growths spreading upwards from the point of contact between the cement and the back of your aquarium. From the base of each of these a small quantity of porridge-like material will sometimes run down to the aquarium floor. This material is working out of the cement, and is far more noticeable when the aquarium is first filled with sea water. If you prefer to fill it with fresh water first, the trouble sometimes does not develop. However, it is of little consequence; after a fortnight it can be scraped off with the finger and no more should appear.

We have kept prawns in a freshly cemented tank without any apparent discomfort to them, but this is not really advisable.

The cement should be mixed at the rate of one part cement to one part of sand, and the sand should be as fine as possible. Moulding sand, such as used in foundries for casting lead, is ideal but, failing a supply of this, ordinary sharp sand can be well sifted. Mix thoroughly before adding water. Finally add sufficient water to make the cement into a whipped-cream consistency, and you will find this ideal for working. If the mix is too dry it will not hold the rocks in place. Expert brick-layers will prefer to use the correct tools, but we have found that an ordinary table knife (some aquarists are quite un-scrupulous) is ideal. Providing it is washed immediately after use, no harm is done, either to the knife or to your reputation.

Be sure to fill in all irregularities behind the rocks as you cement them in place, and this is best done by placing a large portion of cement on the rock face to be secured to the tank. Press this rock against the tank and remove the surplus cement that squeezes out.

When all rocks have been securely cemented into place, the cement 'ties' between the rocks can be camouflaged by pressing some large sand grains into them, and the odd empty seashell such as a limpet or winkle can be stuck there for effect. If some of the exposed cemented surfaces are large, a quick and efficient

Page 33 (*above*) Purple-tipped sea urchin attached to the front glass of a small tank; (*below*) close-up look at a green shore crab

Page 34 (above) The sea hare is an interesting sea slug, well worth a place in a small aquarium; (below) a grey sea slug approaches a snakelocks anemone, which it will then eat

method of covering them with sand is to throw small handfuls at them. Providing sufficient force is used the result will be quite pleasing—but always do this job out in the garden or you will have to spend the next half-hour brushing up sand grains that have ricocheted all over the floor.

Pure cement protruding from rockwork is always unsightly, but after a few months under sea water it will soon develop a growth of weed and blend with the natural rocks.

FLOOR COVERING

The choice of sand will be to some extent governed by the material available in your own neighbourhood, but this should never prevent your using more decorative sand if it can be obtained. The term 'more decorative' does not include mixtures of fancy-coloured chipped glass and brilliantly coloured manufactured sands. Such mixtures merely detract from the natural beauty of the creatures you are keeping and eventually become an eyesore.

When deciding on the amount of sand required it is well to remember that a thick covering of more than a ¼in will inevitably lead to trouble in the form of black deposits. These deposits not only take oxygen out of the water, but look unsightly and will soon develop a most unpleasant smell. Thick layers of sand always lack oxygen and water circulation cannot cope with such a depth. Moreover, fragments of food soon disappear under the sand and decompose.

The most successful covering is one that just obscures the base of the tank, and if the odd crab disturbs this layer and exposes the tank floor it is an easy matter to redistribute it by using a glass rod or small stick. It is better to do this regularly than develop other troubles later through using too thick a layer of sand.

The particle size of the sand is also important. Very fine sand tends to bed down tightly but will be disturbed by actively moving creatures and tend to cloud the water a few inches above the tank floor. The ideal mixture is one in which the sand particles range in size from a match-head to a small pea. With fine sand the discharged matter from your sea creatures will never settle on the bottom if you have a good circulation of air or water. There is nothing to 'bind' it down. With a coarser mixture these waste matters tend to settle between the larger grains, whence they can be readily siphoned off at regular intervals.

Many aquarists delight in cleaning out their tanks, and regularly take out all the sand and give it a good wash under a running tap. From the smell of such sand they wrongly conclude, 'It's a good job I did that.' The fault lies in the sand being too thick, and experience will show that in small tanks the cleaning of sand should never require attention more than once a year at most, if then.

Whilst on the subject of sand, mention must be made of the pros and cons of sloping the floor, either to front or back. It is contended that with a floor sloping towards the back of the tank, all waste products tend to collect in one place where they can then be more easily siphoned off. Whilst this may be so in theory, it so often happens that small pockets of decay are set up that would never have begun if the sand were level. After all, most aquarists will be prepared to spend a few hours a week working on their tanks, and indeed many are positively disappointed if there is nothing to do.

Air diffusers can look unsightly if left bare on the sand. Try using a whelk shell, and by boring a hole to take the airline the diffuser can be hidden within. Admittedly the air bubbles may look a little incongruous, but at least you are using natural material for camouflage purposes, and this is surely warranted.

FEATURES

Under this heading one should include all the fandangles beloved of the traditional goldfish bowl. Let us hope that no serious aquarist will smother his tank with gnomes fishing underwater, or imitation divers. Providing great care is excercised, however, some features can be introduced and with skill they can be most effective. The great point to bear in mind is that the effect to be aimed at should be merely suggested and not, in fact, created.

For instance, if you must have a wreck, do not try to construct a hull of a ship with gaping wounds from new wood, nor, for that matter, from old timber. Actual construction is not required, but with a little artistry the desired effect can be attained by collecting a few scraps of driftwood from the shore or river bank. Let them dry, and then break pieces off, leaving rough edges, until you have two or three pieces that can be so placed as to give the effect required. If you hide one end behind a rock, it will look as if there really is a wreck half-concealed. But somehow a tank usually looks better without them, unless it is of a size comparable with those found in a public aquarium.

Sometimes the aquarist will decide that an odd stone placed on the sand will add to the effect of the general layout. This is permissible provided it is moved quite regularly or else cemented to the base of the tank. Loose stones invite decaying deposits and provide a bank for trouble.

LIGHTING

There are many and diverse opinions concerning the correct type and quantity of light to be used for marine aquaria. Primarily one should bear in mind the question of cost. Fluorescent tubes may well cost more to install but once you have them they will give far greater light for far less money.

As an instance, two 4ft long tanks can be lit by a single 4ft 80 watt tube placed 3ft above the water level. Five 2ft long tanks can be illuminated by the same size tube placed 18in above the water level. This latter will of course give more intense illumination over the centre and less at the sides, but by carefully sorting your specimens you can place the light-loving creatures where it is brightest.

Tube lighting of this type will give you a fairly good growth of weed which will not become excessive if the total amount of light-hours do not exceed twelve per day.

Ordinary bulbs are ideal for a single tank and there is something to be said for the play of shadow that results, whereas with the tubes you will get a shadowless light.

Throughout this chapter the emphasis has been on the desirability of creating a natural home for your animals. There can be no better instructor than the rock pools where they live. If you can recreate in miniature the beauty of a natural rock pool, you will have accomplished the perfection that is to be aimed at—an aquarium that is harmonious both in concept and execution.

4

FILTRATION, CIRCULATION
AND AERATION

TYPES OF EQUIPMENT

It is hoped that most marine aquarists will secure a good air pump so that the water can be both circulated and aerated, with filtration progressing meanwhile.

If, however, you feel it is not yet time for that, an improvised system can make use of a small reservoir. For this set-up you will need something in the nature of a large wooden barrel, a plastic bucket or small cistern so that extra sea water can be stored at a higher elevation than the surface of your tank. The idea is to keep this container filled and to allow the water to trickle slowly from it into the aquarium, thence by way of an overflow into a second container below the aquarium (Fig 3).

It works quite well, provided the water passes through a filtration medium between the outflow and the bottom container. It is better still if you can filter the water before filling the reservoir, but this must be done each time. The entire apparatus is kept working by merely transferring water from the bottom to the top reservoir. Once a day is sufficient, but do not expect such good results as if you used an air pump.

Airlines are often a problem, especially when they have to conduct air over fairly long distances. Although the correct rubber tubing is best, it is also expensive, especially when several yards are involved. So often the aquarist tries to secure tubing of the correct bore, but this is not at all essential for, as shown in

Fig 4, it is a simple matter to adapt tubing of any bore for use as an airline. For instance, you may use a draught-excluder, second-hand rubber airline such as is used on milking machines, or rubber 'piping'.

Wherever air cocks are fitted, the continual pressure will eventually perish the rubber at the point where the cock is attached, and therefore watch this point for any air leaks. It is a good plan to attach these cocks as near to the end of the tubing as convenient, so that when a leak does occur, you can easily

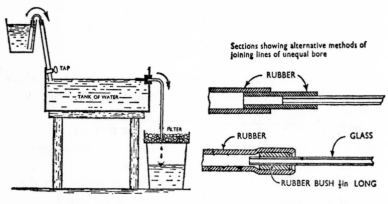

Sections showing alternative methods of joining lines of unequal bore

RUBBER

RUBBER   GLASS

RUBBER BUSH ½in LONG

TAP

TANK OF WATER

FILTER

Fig 3   Bucket reservoir   *Fig 4*   Jointing of airlines

cut away a short end and not waste tubing. By the same token always have a loop of a foot or so in your airline to allow for future requirements.

If you intend to run a number of tanks from a large aerator, the best method is to have a length of plastic hosepipe of ½in diameter running from the pump straight along to the end of the last tank. This length can then be cut above each tank and a metal or plastic junction-piece inserted, and to this is attached your airline for the tank. Plastic junction-pieces can be bought quite cheaply, or made from lengths of plastic tubing as shown in Fig 5. These short lengths are stuck together with any good aero glue.

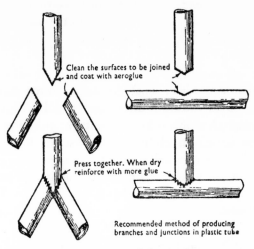

Clean the surfaces to be joined and coat with aeroglue

Press together. When dry reinforce with more glue

Recommended method of producing branches and junctions in plastic tube

Fig 5   Jointing of plastic tube

COLLECTION OF SEA WATER

In the majority of cases, perhaps, the marine aquarist will not find himself able to obtain unlimited supplies of sea water. His available supply must be safeguarded and used to the best possible advantage. Even those more fortunate folk who have easy access to the sea soon find the transport of large quantities becomes irksome. The following 'systems' are therefore arranged in distinct groups so that the individual can more easily decide the best system for his particular situation. Since few amateur aquarists will have the good fortune to possess a pump and pipeline into the sea, no attempt to describe such an Eldorado will be made. In Chapter 15 on public aquaria an outline is given for those interested.

If you are able to get to the sea you will probably prefer to use real sea water rather than make it artificially. It's heavy stuff, so a light container makes carrying easier. Polythene laundry bags placed inside a bucket have the advantage that you can tie the top and thus prevent your sea water slopping over. An ordinary cardboard carton such as is used in the delivery of bulk groceries makes an excellent light container with a thick polythene bag as a liner; with stout cord to keep the box in one piece, it will survive a number of visits to the sea.

FILTRATION

To filter or not to filter? That question is often debated, for those in favour of filtration know the crystal clarity of clean water, whereas the other school maintain (and correctly) that filtering removes too much life from the water. If we take two extremes, the point can be illustrated.

Firstly, then, an aquarist with almost unlimited supplies of water, one who can obtain it just whenever he desires. The water he gets will not, however, always be the same, and only those who have collected it where the surf is rolling in can appreciate how murky it may be. Presuming it is essential to collect water from a surfy sea, the first thing to do is leave the bottles in a cool place for twenty-four hours, so that much of the silt can settle. In a two-gallon jar, it is not uncommon to find a 1mm-thick layer on the bottom after settlement, and the clearer water should on no account be poured off. This will only stir up the last half gallon, and you are right back where you started. Siphon it off and make certain that the end of your tube is well clear of the settled silt, and get the siphon going first time with a good strong suck. Admittedly a throatful of salt water is not exactly stimulating, but neither is the frustration of waiting a further day for the freshly stirred 'soup' to settle.

If you want to get things moving more quickly, make a small filter like that shown in Fig 6 and pour the water straight into the tank.

Frequently the water you have collected will be fairly clear, and this can be poured straight into the tank without filtering, for in this way any plankton present will go where they are wanted—into the aquarium.

But, the majority of aquarists will need to filter the old tank water. The same method of collecting sea water applies, and it must be allowed to settle.

There are various methods of filtering that can be used, and

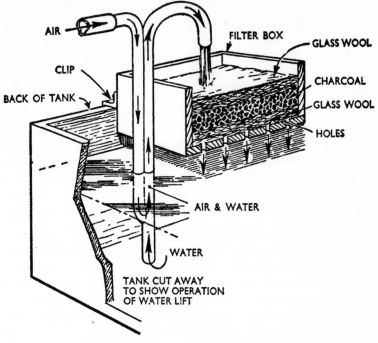

Fig 6 A small filter

there is no doubt that a little thought and experiment could evolve new ones. Primarily an external filter has everything to commend it, for the waste products are being carried out of the aquarium and cannot easily be re-absorbed. With internal filters a certain amount of silt is 'washed off' the glass wool by passing fish and foraging crabs.

Most filters used by amateurs are of the air-lift type and work by bubbles of air lifting drops of water as shown in Fig 6. An air-lift of this kind can be purchased cheaply at any aquarist supplier, and providing the air control is well adjusted, it will lift a good quantity of water into the filter bed. As an example, a 2ft tank with fairly cloudy water can be cleared in forty-eight hours. On the other hand, if you have such a filter already fitted and providing nothing 'crawls away and dies', the water will remain crystal clear for an indefinite period.

The adjustment of air to these filters is often quite delicate, and it is wrong to suppose that the more air there is available, the better the flow of water. A good steady flow is far better than the spluttering upheaval that follows an overdose of pressure. An extra strong air pressure usually blows out through the bottom of the air-lift tube, or else delivers a steady flow of air into the aquarium cover. So you should exercise moderation and adjust the control cock carefully.

There is a wide choice of filter mediums available, some cheap and others costly, but one of the easiest is without doubt glass wool and charcoal. The glass wool can be obtained from any reliable pharmacist, and even if he does not stock it he will always get it for you, although if there is an aquarist shop near by try there first. Place the glass wool in a 1in layer over the bottom of the filter, then add a 1in layer of granulated charcoal, and finally cover this with a further layer of glass wool. Make sure the charcoal is granulated, because the powdered kind is useless and very quickly fills your aquarium with black dust.

A filter of this type, working a 2ft tank, will need a top layer of glass wool changed about once a fortnight, and the charcoal can be replaced every other month. At the end of the first week of use, the glass wool can be cleaned by washing it under a flowing tap, but be sure to keep the wool loose, or it will bind tightly together and be of no further use. Sometimes a batch can be washed a second and even a third time, but for really efficient filtration fresh glass wool should be used each time.

We have made no mention of limestone chips. What about our pH? I suppose if you really must stick pH papers into the water and have sleepless nights over increased acidity, it is as well to place a few limestone chips on top of the glass wool. Frankly, we have never found this necessary.

Sand makes quite a good filtering medium, but is very much slower than those we have mentioned. You must use a fine sand, and this does tend to clog up, while its tighter particle packing cuts down the water-flow. With small amounts of water it is quite satisfactory.

In filters where the water drips through holes in the bottom of the filter box, the sand can be retained by placing glass wool as a bottom layer. This must be watched, of course, because the glass wool tends to clog up and the material should be changed every fortnight so that the water-flow through the filter is not impeded. Only those who have had blocked filters running over the top rim will appreciate how much accumulated filth is carried back into the tank when this happens.

If sea water is very valuable to you, and the collection of a fresh supply means a long journey, the best safety precaution is the use of several filters. Either have two filter boxes, each with two air-lifts attached, or one filter box with four air-lifts. Any good air pump will give sufficient pressure for the work, and you will have perfectly clear, safe water.

Sub-sand biological filters, commercially produced, are another possibility. These are buried beneath a 1in deep layer of sand in the bottom of the tank. The tank sand is used as the filtration medium and as the sand becomes biologically active most of the impurities are absorbed.

Circulation pumps can be obtained from pet shops and aquarists' stores. Find one suitable for your size of tank. The water is circulated through a filter pack specially provided, which has to be renewed periodically and will give you perfectly clear, well-filtered water. This type of circulation ensures that a large volume of water is in continual circulation and being returned in a cleansed condition as all impurities are left behind in the pack.

Filter pumps need not be left on for twenty-four hours a day; generally speaking, four- to five-hour spells should suffice. The handyman can easily rig up a time-clock that will do the whole job automatically.

When ordering one of these pumps stipulate marine, as a fresh water model is also available.

AERATION

Most of the creatures we keep in marine tanks benefit from a circulation of water, and the easiest way to ensure this, apart from using a water pump which has to be non-contaminating, is by good aeration.

Many of our leading aquarists maintain that aeration causes gas blisters in fish, and such opinions have been based upon actual experience. Our own experience, however, does not bear this out, especially in small aquaria where the water is not circulated from a main reservoir.

There was a period when we experimented quite deliberately to find whether fine bubbles or large bubbles were best. From the observed results there was little or no difference, providing the large bubbles were emitted rapidly. It is our opinion that the whole question of aeration rests primarily on the amount of circulation caused by the uprush of the air. This keeps the surface water moving and constantly changing, and it is here that the real absorption of oxygen will occur.

The incidental effect of this circulation is no less important than the value of the increased oxygen made available. I remember how this was first brought vividly to my notice. A small two-spot goby, which I had had for several months, used to rest inside an empty otter-shell. Some days he was particularly active, but on other days he remained for long periods out of sight. Then due to a mechanical failure of the large aerating pump that supplied all the tanks, I was without air for three days. During that entire spell the goby remained inactive, but as soon as the air came on he was out swimming again. He had not been inactive due to lack of oxygen, but simply because there was no flow of water. Next time you are around the rocks watch the reaction of prawns to the change of tide; ask fishermen whether the tide affects fishing, and watch fish in tide-rips.

Try this experiment yourself. Turn off the circulation system, and soon after the air bubbles stop rising you will notice that all movement of the water within the tank ceases. Within an hour or less, most of the inhabitants will also have become quiescent. The fish will be at rest on the floor sand, or float quietly somewhere between the surface and the sand; the crabs will be motionless, crouched under their favourite rock; prawns cease to move and go into the nearest corner, or rest alongside the side of the tank. Only the sedentary or semi-sedentary animals will remain feeding.

Now switch on the circulation. Within a very few minutes everything begins to move once more, and the first signs of action come from the creatures adjusting their positions to face the oncoming current of water. There is no doubt that water movement in an aquarium is a first essential for any successful tank. After that you will no longer debate the value of aeration, and can realise that its purpose is not 'air for air's sake', but simply to increase circulation. Good marine aquaria, like good periodicals, have a steady and widespread circulation.

5

MAINTENANCE OF THE TANKS

The maintenance of a successful marine aquarium demands little more than plain commonsense application of a few simple rules. Normally an aquarium should remain perfectly clear for a number of years, without any drastic and complete changes of water.

The greatest enemy to clean, fresh sea water is decaying animal or vegetable matter, and it really is surprising how quickly a tank will 'go off' once trouble sets in. Since prevention is better than cure, it is a good plan to ensure that all uneaten food is removed about two hours after feeding your stock. This can be done by using a siphon, and passing the outlet through a filter which will trap the waste and allow the clear water to settle in a container below.

In a small tank, say up to 3ft in length and less than 2ft deep, a glass tube will do the job very tidily with little loss of water. The method is as follows: Hold the tube in your right hand with the first finger over the open end at the top. Lower the tube into the water until the open end at the bottom is over the material to be picked up, and then release your finger. The water rushes up the tube and takes with it the rubbish. Replace your finger, lift out the tube and again release the finger, allowing rubbish to run into your waste can. If those instructions sound like a rather complicated conjuring trick, try it first and you will find it is far more simple than it sounds.

Food is not the only source of contamination, however, and careful watch must be kept on any shellfish or small hermit crabs, and especially anemones. Of these three, the shellfish are the most likely to cause trouble, so watch out for the odd one that settles down in one place for a few days; unless it is a limpet, the chances are it is dead, and building up a little trouble for you. You can easily touch it occasionally with a glass tube, and as long as there is a reaction it is living, but beware the shellfish that never moves when it is touched. Small hermit crabs will sometimes leave their shells when ill, and crawl away to some corner before dying. If you spot an empty hermit shell, find its late owner.

Anemones are usually very hardy animals, but some have a habit of dying so slowly that it is difficult to observe until sudden decomposition sets in. A dead anemone often looks so like one that is behaving in the normal manner that only the smell when it is removed convinces the aquarist of his suspicions. And we know of nothing as offensive as a dead anemone.

Plumose anemones have a habit of sloughing-off long mucous-like slime trails that are very nearly transparent. These trails settle on the bottom of the aquarium and will collect all manner of rubbish on their adhesive coils. Remove at once, and the best way is to use a siphon and suck them off the living anemone before they drop.

Before introducing whelks into a tank, let them crawl around a stone jar for a day or so. The reason for this is that whelks, after travelling for a few hours either out of water or in restricted water space, very soon collect a good deal of slime on their large foot. If you introduce them right away into your aquarium that slime will be left all over the glass or on the sandy bottom. Wherever it is left it is difficult to remove, so let them settle down first.

Once you develop a routine for the introduction of new specimens and the removal of food, you have progressed a long way towards a crystal-clear aquarium.

It must be appreciated that crystal clarity, although a desirable goal where the fish are concerned, is by no means the criterion of success where filter feeders are concerned. If after some weeks your aquarium has become clear, and you have it set up as a

49

community tank containing various creatures, give your filter feeders an occasional 'holiday'. Move a thin piece of wood over the sand at the bottom of the aquarium, and so disturb some of the sediment that has settled there in spite of all your care. Turn on the air a little more fiercely so that the sediment is kept moving, and you will find all your plumose anemones opening right up to catch the suspended particles, whilst fan-worms and mussels and their like will all take their toll of the floating food that you have released. If this is done just before you go to bed most of the silt will have cleared by the morning, and the air can then be reduced.

Such treatment also tends to release some of the minerals that have been retained by the silt, and in a very small way helps to maintain your sea water at its correct mineral level.

EVAPORATION

Even when glass covers are provided, a certain amount of evaporation will still occur, and after a month or more in summertime the water level begins to drop. Make up to your 'water level' mark with fresh tap water. Remember that only water vapour has gone, and the salts have been left, so if you add sea water you will merely be concentrating it still further. Topping-up should be done as often as once a week during warm weather to prevent any sudden changes in the salinity of the water.

You will often find a rim of salt on your glass cover, where the tiny bubbles from your aerator have burst and splashed sea water on to the glass. Remember that this salt is no longer in the water, so try and regulate the air supply to avoid too vigorous aeration.

LIMING

Some aquarists delight in testing the water for its pH. If you must do this (and believe me it is not necessary), use the standard pH papers which give colour readings. If the pH reads as low as 7, then you can add a small amount of dissolved lime as lime

Page 51 (*above*) A crumb-of-bread sponge; (*below*) a snakelocks anemone; this species needs abundant light in order to thrive

Page 52 *(above)* A shoal of mullet; each fish is less than two inches in length; *(below)* if offered whelk shells, blennies will often make one into a home.

water until the acidity is corrected. If limestone is incorporated in your filter system, and renewed every few months, you should have no trouble with acidity. Having maintained perfectly balanced aquaria for very long periods without any artificial aids, we are convinced that the chemistry of sea water is best left untouched in small home aquaria.

SOME HINTS

If the water goes suddenly from crystal clarity to a misty whiteness, look for the 'body' that is providing food for the bacteria that form that cloud. Remove it and aerate freely for twenty-four hours.

Do not play around with your sea water once it has settled down.

If you are one of the unfortunate individuals who must 'do things' to your aquarium, try sitting in front of it. Next, record your observations and make a few sketches. In this way you will find a new interest—and the aquarium will improve.

Remember that maintenance of a good marine aquarium takes very little time, and it is only the poor ones that need much attention. Cut your troubles by observing the few simple rules in this chapter, and you will soon discover that not only is it a beautiful aquarium you now have, but more important perhaps, you have plenty of time to watch the interesting habits of the creatures you are keeping in good health.

6

COLLECTING SPECIMENS

The collecting work carried out by the average marine aquarist will depend upon his nearness to the sea, but there is no doubt that this work can be one of the most interesting aspects of the hobby. No greater variety of specimens could be found in any habitat; no other form of collecting requires the skill needed for discovering the creatures of the sea in their own homes.

Camouflage and concealment are the two protective cloaks that cover the living creatures of rock pools; let your shadow fall across the water and all movement within the pool will cease instantly; penetrate the surface water with a clumsy thrust of the net, and once more everything living in the pool will 'freeze'. The real 'know-how' of collecting is acquired only after long experience, but we can with patience learn to collect many interesting forms in an occasional trip lasting no more than two hours.

Briefly the rules are as follows:

1. Check your tide tables. Make sure the tide is well down the beach before you start, and if possible choose a spring tide, ie at full and new moon, as then the ebb exposes areas normally covered by the water.
2. Be sure to take sufficient buckets and polythene bags. How often do we find insufficient storage space in our box or bag, and have to make a choice between two particularly good specimens?

3. Be quiet.
4. Keep in such a position that your shadow will not fall across the water.
5. Move slowly if wading.

Now take a look at these respective points individually. Tide tables can be purchased at all seaside resorts and in bookshops; tide times are notified in local newspapers.

Spring tides occur every fortnight, and in between there are the neap tides, when comparatively little tidal movement takes place. When on a collecting expedition try and get to the seashore at least an hour before low tide. In this way you will be able to follow the tide down on its last few feet of ebb and find many creatures that have not yet 'hidden up'. A flooding spring tide rises quickly, and the collector who arrives late will find the laminaria zone rapidly disappearing. The lowest spring tides occur three days after new and full moons, and the best collecting period is from one day before new and full moon to four days after.

It is a good idea to make some sort of collecting box as shown in Fig 7 and this can be adapted in a variety of ways according to the containers you have readily available. The question of packing the catch will always loom large, but generally speaking, keep the larger creatures such as crabs in a separate compartment well packed in weed. Water is not required, unless specimens have to spend many hours within the container. If you wish to carry small fish home, place about $\frac{1}{2}$in of water in the bottom of the container. *Never fill it*, for it is a misconception to imagine that the more water you have the happier will be the fish within. In the small quantity the fish will remain splashing about and aerate the water themselves. As a matter of fact many *shore* fishes travel better in damp seaweed than water. A clear distinction must be made between shore fishes and deeper-water species, for these latter must have a plentiful water supply when transported, and the water should also be aerated. The reason for this is simply that species living offshore are used to living permanently in water. Rockpool and shore fish, however, are

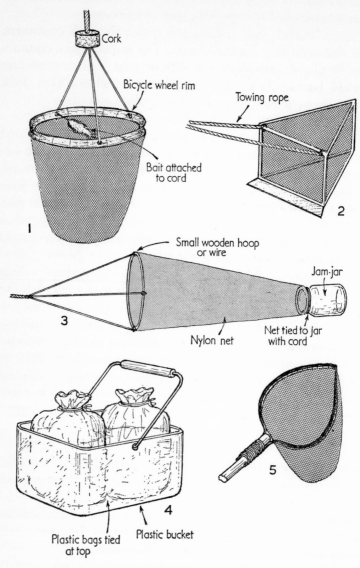

Cork

Bicycle wheel rim

Towing rope

Bait attached
to cord

1

2

Small wooden hoop
or wire

Jam·jar

3

Nylon net

Net tied to jar
with cord

Plastic bags tied
at top

Plastic bucket

4

5

Fig 7 Collecting apparatus: 1 drop net; 2 dredge; 3 plankton net;
4 collecting bucket; 5 prawning net

conditioned to being left 'dry' by the receding tide, and are therefore adapted to cope with such conditions.

Never crowd your collection together in small containers, for this invariably leads to losses. The more robust creatures can be placed underneath the delicate ones, and extreme care should be exercised when handling sea urchins. They look tough, but are easily injured internally.

If some particularly good specimen is discovered by chance when you just happened to be walking along the shore, a good emergency pack can be made from a plastic container or ice-cream carton—such usually abound on the shore in summertime.

One last brief but important suggestion. It is better to have your collecting box slung by a strap from your shoulders than to try to carry it in one hand. There are plenty of times when the shore collector will need all available limbs to keep upright on the slippery weeds.

The business of quietness and shadows is perhaps a little obvious to go into in detail, but sufficient to say that fish like the two-spot goby will take immediate cover if your shadow falls across the water. Also, always remember, when wading, that your movements travel ahead of you in the form of sound waves and pressure waves, and these can quickly be detected by the creatures you are trying to catch. The active ones will take cover if you make undue disturbance, so make slow, steady movements.

NETS

Most collectors think in terms of nets, although experience often shows that hand collecting is far more successful. Types of net are shown in Fig 7.

THE PRAWN NET. If used skilfully during late spring and summer and into the autumn this will take wrasse, prawns, crabs, mullet and various other occasional specimens.

Choose a pool where the wrack hangs down in proctective curtains from rock ledges that overhang the sea bed. It is behind this screen that life is most abundant. Prawns will be resting upside down on the surface of that ledge; crabs lurk in the weed and in the narrow fissures behind; small wrasse hug the rock-face; a host of fish find refuge in this shaded underwater jungle.

Put your net into the water quietly and move it along slowly, getting right under the ledge. Keep it moving at a steady speed, but if it gets jammed against some unseen obstacle pull it up quickly or your catch will be gone. Wherever there is weed hanging down, sweep your net through it, and get into every corner possible, and for that reason the heart-shaped net is ideal, for the point will go where a larger ring would never penetrate.

If you want shrimps for food then the net shown in Fig 8 is best, for the wide front bar scrapes along the sand and disturbs these creatures that tend to hug the sandy bottom. Shrimp nets should only be used at low-tide on a sandy shore, and if your shore is well sheltered with zostera weed growing there you may well catch small cuttlefish and a variety of young fish.

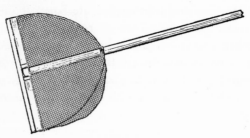

Fig 8 Shrimp net

DROP NETS. When baited with fish these are ideal for collecting at night, but seldom give reward during daylight. The illustration in Fig 7 shows how they are made, and the bait cord can be seen stretching across the centre of the net. Secure a piece of fish skeleton (obtained from the local fishmonger) to this cord and tie it securely or else the crabs will tear it free on the first haul.

Drop nets can be used from piers, harbour walls, rock ledges, overhanging water of over 6ft in depth, or from boats out in deeper water when the nets should be dropped over rocky reefs or between rocks. Always lower the net down so that it rests on the sea bed close to the wall or rocks, for it is here that the specimens you are after will be abundant. You can easily see why this is if you watch the water from some harbour steps, as the tide rises after dark. Flash your torch downwards and you will find abundance of life crawling and swimming against the tide-drifted weed, and a host of tiny flashing lights sparkle in the depths as the prawns' eyes reflect your light.

But to return to our net. Lower it down and then leave it on the bottom for a full five minutes at least, and ten minutes will bring better results, for it gives time for various specimens to get the scent of your bait and to get into your net. When you haul up, do so with a smooth pulling motion and keep the net moving until it breaks the surface. If you do not keep that net moving, many of the more actively swimming creatures will be out of the net before it breaks surface.

Before using this type of net, it is as well to check over the ground for unseen snags. Projecting timbers, mooring chains, mooring ropes, jagged and overhanging rocks can all snare your net when you try to pull it up, and once that happens the catch will have gone. Another small but important point concerns your lamp; be sure to place it well away from the edge of the place where you are working, or one of those nights the outrunning rope will take it into the depths. The choice of baits for these nets is wide, and personal experience alone will prove the best for your own locality, but plaice skeletons are a useful bait and can be obtained at most fish shops.

PLANKTON NETS. These can be made quite cheaply from a good quality, small-meshed nylon net curtain material. Choose a formal squared pattern and do not go in for fancy 'rose' patterns, as such material frequently has weaker threads where motifs are worked into the general pattern, thus making it more vulnerable. Fig 7 shows a typical plankton net. The jam jar can be fixed to the net by means of a piece of stout cord; in this way it can readily be released and the catch emptied into your collecting jar.

There are various methods of using such nets, but first and foremost it must be emphasised that speed of movement is the reason for disappointingly small catches. Always move the net slowly, for even the more lively forms of plankton can be taken with a 3ft diameter net towed at less than 2 miles an hour. Tow nets bring their richest catches during the months of May, June, and July, but they can be used at any time of the year and will always yield some interesting specimens.

First let us imagine you intend to work from a small rowing boat. Having got under way and with the end of the tow-line secured to the rowlock, lower the net quietly into the water, letting it stream out astern until the rope goes tight. Now all that is required is to keep the net moving through the water as slowly as possible for a distance of about a quarter of a mile. By this time a good collection of swimming planktonic forms should be in it.

If it is June, you will find large numbers of sea gooseberries swimming around in your jar. Whilst these are difficult to keep for any length of time, they are worth observing, for they are hungry creatures and will catch and devour smaller plankton forms very readily. At the same time of year you will certainly find a variety of post-larval fish in your catch, and whilst they make good food for many aquarium fish such as blennies and gobies, they can only be kept if you are prepared to work hard in securing the necessary food for them. If you decide to try and rear a few of them for observation, you will have to supply plenty of plankton as food when their yolk-sacs are absorbed.

A second method of using this kind of net is to allow it to stream out in a strong tidal current, such as is found in a river estuary. If the tide is very strong you may need to add a piece of lead tubing to the rim of the net in order to get sufficient depth, as the strain of the tide tends to lift the net to the surface.

One point must be remembered when collecting plankton; when the day is very sunny and bright they will be found deeper down, but in the evening they rise towards the surface and will be caught at shallower depths. It has been found by biologists that plankton show very definite preferences for light of a certain well-defined intensity, and so it should be deep by day and shallow at night.

THE DREDGE. The last type of net is the dredge (Fig 7). Whatever material is used, it should be heavy gauge, because the weight is necessary to keep the dredge on the bottom and to help it to dig into the sea bed. The front bar is so made that it slopes downwards towards the sand and thereby cuts further downwards as the net is towed along.

When one of these nets is first used, it is well to test it out over known ground that is free from rocks and other obstructions. Good places to try such nets are over sandy beaches a short distance out from the limit of low tide, and around the smooth sand that often outlines the jagged inshore rocks. If you know of a good reef and can judge its contours exactly, then it will be rewarding to row right along the very edge of the rocks, for it is here that a rich variety of animal life often hides itself.

Small spider crabs (*Macropodia*) and numerous burrowing shellfish can be dredged along most coastlines, but the importance of knowing your own piece of coast cannot be over-emphasised. It is only by getting to know your ground that you will ever succeed in getting some of those rarer specimens that are so sought after. There is always an element of luck, and the unexpected frequently happens, but to depend upon luck is merely to invite disappointment.

HAND COLLECTING

The seashore naturalist will often find his richest rewards when searching the low-tide levels with no other equipment than his hands. Get down to the shore a couple of hours before low tide, and begin your searching by lifting rocks and looking quickly for the more active creatures that will endeavour to race for new cover. Having made sure that you have missed none of these, look more carefully at the sand and weed beneath the rock and on the under-surfaces of the rock itself. Always return the rock to its original position, and so save the great population that live on and beneath it from death in the sunlight and desiccation by the wind.

As the tide draws towards the lowest levels, especially if it is the time of spring tides, the real hunting-grounds become exposed. Here among the rich weed-covered rocks, beneath those weed-curtained ledges, and in the cool dark fissures that run between, a wealth of specimens will be found. Sponges cover the rocks if the place is well sheltered, and a rich variety of starfish will be seen. Sea anemones too, like the dahlia anemone (*Tealia felina*), are larger than those species higher up the shore and can be collected here. Here, too, the variety of shellfish is greater, for you are standing on the verge of the two worlds—the seashore and the deeper sea.

It is not easy to give advice on how to collect by hand in this region, as the greatest asset is a keen pair of eyes and just a little patience and observation. Always remember sea creatures are masters of camouflage, and it often happens that the beginner stares so amazed at the variety of life around him that he fails to see the rare creature disguised among the fringes of the weed.

Apart from the rocks, other good collecting places are pier piles, harbour walls, and river estuaries. All these places will reveal their own particular life, and it is surprising the number of animals that gather around the base of a pier pile, just beyond the limit of low tide. Use a pair of thigh waders, or if you intend to do a lot of shore collecting you can invest in a rubber suit and spend a little extra time snorkelling along the edge of the tide.

In certain areas the low spring tides occur at midday and midnight. Then midnight is the ideal time for collecting, for with a paraffin pressure lamp it is possible to see so much more easily. Gone are the distractions of daylight hunting, gone the small boys with shrimp nets and loudly splashing feet disturbing the quiet of rock pools. Now, under the dark sky all the creatures of the pools and seashore are moving freely on their various journeys, and many that by day would be found far inside rock crevices are now strolling boldly through the open spaces of a large pool. Each small pool is lined with the glistening eyes of prawns, and vari-coloured crabs feed on the pool bed. Perhaps the idea of missing sleep does not appeal at first reading. That is a great pity, for the shore at night is a place apart, and your probing light will reveal so much of interest that you will be sorry to see the flooding tide moving inwards across the sand and rock pools.

OTHER SOURCES

Many aquarists will want to obtain specimens from deeper water, or at times when a particular species is perhaps not so numerous along the shore. Trawlermen will nearly always help out providing you do not expect too much too soon. Their job is a busy one, and sorting their catch takes time, so do not expect them to bring home the creature you have asked for on the first trip.

Local crabbers get a variety of interesting creatures in their crab and lobster pots, and such colourful things as squat lobsters, resplendent in red and blue stripes, make an almost tropical brilliance in a small tank. Small octopuses sometimes find their way into these pots, and providing their tentacles are not more than 6in across they will settle down in a 3ft tank. In their season, the scallop dredgers are a useful source of many burrowing creatures, although the chief trouble here is that their large-mesh steel dredges allow most of the smaller creatures to escape, and too often those still held captive are badly damaged. Dredging of this type is heavy work and only the tougher shellfish survive a mauling in the dredge.

Collecting vessels, making regular trips, are activities run in Britain by the Marine Biological Association, and there is normally a good supply of interesting live species for sale.

7

THE INVERTEBRATES

Sponges, Jellyfish, Corals, Anemones and Worms

Some sort of orderly arrangement is necessary if we are to consider the varied forms of life that can be kept in marine aquaria. In this book we have split them into two main groups, Vertebrates and Invertebrates. The latter, the animals without backbones, are so frequently overlooked that few people realise they comprise about 95 per cent of the species of the animal kingdom! Their diverse ways of life are no less startling than their numbers.

In the sea the invertebrates range from the simplest single-celled flagella to the lobsters and crabs. As they progress in development we find more and more specialisation in their various organs and increasing degrees of complexity in structure. Thus we start with details about the simpler forms of life, such as sponges, and progress to more complex ones such as the lobster. Finally, fish as vertebrate animals will be dealt with.

SPONGES (*Porifera*)

Some distance down the shore, towards the limit of low tides and beneath the weed-hung rocks, you will find the sponges. Sheltered from the drying effect of the sun and wind they are usually attached to the under-surface of rocks, and their volcano-like openings point downward to the pools below. Yellow, red, orange, and green, they are so varied in colour that in

64

sheltered bays and coves, or better still estuaries, your choice is unlimited.

They can be removed by separating them from the rock surface with a sharp knife, and you should pack them in damp seaweed for transporting home. In estuaries you will often find sponges growing on the wrack, but for aquarium use these are not particularly suitable because the weed decays too soon and will foul your water.

Sponges can be kept with varying degrees of success—sometimes they will live for months, and at other times they die and decay soon after introduction to the tank. There is no doubt that they thrive better in water that has a certain amount of suspended matter in it; being filter feeders they will not live for long in filtered water.

The reason for this is obvious if you look carefully at the structure of a sponge under a magnifying glass. You will see innumerable tiny holes pitting the entire surface, with intermittent larger and volcano-like mounds. The sponge is an animal and requires food, and it is through these tiny holes that a continuous current of sea water is drawn into the 'body', where specialised cells extract the tiny fragments of food in the water. The filtered water is then passed out through the larger opening (see plate p 51).

In small aquaria sponges will add colour and interest, especially when you explain to visitors that they are animals. The larger sponges, similar in shape to the ordinary bathroom sponge and trawled up in deeper water, will not survive in small aquaria, but their crevices are a happy hunting ground for the collector.

Sponges must be closely watched for signs of decay. This is normally first seen by a change of colour. For instance, the crumb-of-bread sponge (*Halichondria panicea*), which is normally yellow when living, will turn a patchy green when dying—and few sea animals foul the water quicker than a dead sponge.

They can be kept with most other sea animals, but not with the sea lemon (*Archidoris britannica*) as this creature browses on sponges as food. Since the sea lemon is often abundant in late spring, and its egg ribbons are so interesting to observe, you can always put a piece of sponge in your tank as food when keeping it.

JELLYFISH (*Scyphozoa*)

It is chiefly during the summer months that the vari-coloured jellyfish will be found around the shore, but even then, when collecting good specimens, you should go out to deeper water for here they will be undamaged. There are several ways of collecting them, but the best is to use a large plastic bowl. This is dipped under the jellyfish, so that the animal and a quantity of water are together run into the bowl. This eliminates all handling and further ensures the good condition of your specimen.

Unfortunately for the small-scale aquarist, jellyfish are normally too large for anything less than a 4ft tank, although small ones up to 1½in or so in diameter will live for a while in a 2ft tank.

If examined closely, a typical jellyfish such as *Aurelia* will be found to have a number of fine thread-like filaments hanging down from the outer edge of the bell. These are the stinging polyps which secure food and transfer it to the central feeding polyp which is situated exactly in the centre of the disc. Between this polyp and the stinging ones will be seen reproductive polyps, which at certain times resemble bunches of very young blackcurrant buds. *Aurelia* (*Aurelia aurita*) will not sting you, but beware of the larger purplish *Cyanea*, or the dangerous Portuguese man-of-war (*Physalia physalia*), for these two can raise quite painful weals on the arm or leg.

Feeding jellyfish is no easy matter unless plentiful supplies of plankton are available. Sometimes a specimen will readily take minute pieces of crushed mussel that are stirred into the water, but this feeding method brings in its train the difficulty of water pollution.

CORALS

The most interesting of these, because of its beauty, is the sea fan (*Eunicella verrucosa*). Specimens can be obtained from marine laboratories or occasionally from trawlers and crabbers. Beautifully branched, its orange polyps when fully expanded give it an attractive 'fluffy' appearance that makes an ideal background to any tank. It can be secured to the floor or sides of the tank by sticking its base into a lump of glazing compound and attaching this to the woodwork of the tank, or by attaching it to a sucker disc such as is used to suspend notices in shop windows.

A plentiful supply of suspended matter is essential, and we have found that sea fans live longest in tanks where fish are plentiful, and the water is continually renewed. On the other hand a specimen at present in our possession has lived for six months in a tank of unchanged water, without fish, and is still quite healthy.

First signs of decay are increasing whiteness where once orange was seen, followed by black patches. Once this starts get rid of your sea fan, because it will not survive much longer.

The best way of displaying a sea fan is to place it in a small tank with a large magnifying glass attached to the front glass. A photographic condenser is ideal. The exhibit can then be viewed in close-up, and the individual polyps that make up the colony can be seen to the best advantage.

ANEMONES (*Anthozoa*)

For aquarium purposes these must be divided into two groups, plumose anemones which are plankton feeders, and the long-tentacle types such as opelet and beadlet.

PLUMOSE ANEMONES (*Metridium senile*). These can be found on pier piles and in deeper water attached to old scallop shells and stones. Indeed, plumose anemones can be collected from such places as the shell of a crab, an old rusty anchor, a steel hawser, a wide variety of old shells or even a piece of coal trawled up from the sea bed.

When collecting these from the shore the easiest method is to choose a night when the tide is at lowest springs. Wade out among the pier piles with a paraffin (kerosene) pressure lamp or torch, and with luck your light will pick out the shining but extended body of the anemone draped from some mussel or group of barnacles. By daylight they are not so easily spotted, for their insignificant shape resembles nothing as much as a patch of coloured slime.

Remove them from their attachment by prising one edge of their disc free with the thumb nail and then gently continuing this pressure until the thumb has slid right under the disc and freed the anemone. Carry them home in damp seaweed. When placing them in the aquarium, put them directly on the particular rock where you want them to remain, and for a few hours turn off the air or circulation so that they can settle down without movement. Like all anemones, they will occasionally move about, sometimes as much as a foot in a couple of days, but there is nothing you can do to stop this perfectly natural movement.

Plumose anemones are quite unpredictable in their habits. Some will settle down quickly and within twenty-four hours will be fully expanded, whilst others will refuse to attach themselves to the rocks and remain in untidy 'heaps' on the floor of your tank. Others again after being fully expanded for as long as two months will suddenly—and for no apparent reason—contract into small flat discs that are most uninteresting. These latter can sometimes be awakened by placing a tiny piece of mussel in the central hole where the tentacles are folded in. Another method is to place a mussel in a piece of cotton and to 'wring it out' into the tank close to the anemone. Incidentally this is quite a good way to feed them, although most anemones of the plumose kind will take small pieces of the mantle flesh of mussel if it is placed on the tips of the tentacles. When feeding in this manner, use a glass rod to steer the food on to the tentacles, so that it falls naturally on to the anemone, for the touch of a feeding tong will often make it close up before the food is taken. If mussels are not obtainable, feed with a small piece of filleted fish. Crush the fish up between the fingers and spread it through the water. Whiting or other white fish are ideal, but do not use any oily species.

Another troublesome feature of these anemones is their habit of sloughing off their outer skin. Besides hanging in an untidy frill around their base, this stuff sometimes floats to the surface where it creates further unsightliness. As soon as a piece of this slough is seen, siphon it away from the anemone.

Normally, plumose anemones are seen to best advantage when the lights are switched on after dark, for during darkness they are expanded to their fullest extent, and a specimen that was only 1in tall during the day will be found to be over 3in in the dark.

We have frequently noticed that these anemones thrive in a tank where fish are kept, and that even if the body of the fish contacts them, they will not retract. On the other hand a foraging crab that happens to touch their tentacles causes an immediate contraction and the anemones will remain closed for an hour or more.

Frequently a portion of the basal disc will be seen to open out into a small lobe. The neck of this then contracts until another small anemone is budded off. The entire process takes several days and sometimes several weeks.

Their colour range is wide, but the finest for display are the orange ones. White, grey, orange-brown, and deep brown are other colour varieties.

Extra high temperatures are not appreciated and the incidence of deaths can be correlated to the highness of temperature. They need to be watched if the temperature rises, for a dead anemone will quickly send your water foul, and one that has been dead for two days cannot be removed from the water without sending out a stream of filth. Occasionally the area around the base should be siphoned clean, as dirt collects there and very soon a ring of black sand will denote trouble.

However, their interesting colour and flower-like appearance make plumose anemones useful additions to any tank, and with the few precautions indicated here, they will give little trouble.

SNAKELOCKS OR OPELET ANEMONES (*Anemonia sulcata*). These can be collected in almost any low-tide pool throughout the year, although during the cold winter months they will be found to be very small and colourless. This is due to two possible causes. Firstly, there is little food at such times and this anemone is one that needs plenty of food at not too infrequent intervals.

Secondly, as in its tentacles lives a symbiotic green alga, it needs a good deal of strong sunlight.

If these anemones are collected, placed in a tank lit by tungsten light; fed on mussel flesh, they will grow. If placed in a shaded part of the aquarium they will move into the best-lit portion, which often means the glass front, where they form rather unsightly blobs on the glass. Put them in good light and they will settle down and make a good display. After feeding they excrete a small pellet of undigested food remains, and this will decay rapidly if not removed promptly. Their choice of food is remarkably varied, and whilst their growth is more rapid on mussel, they will take peeled or unpeeled prawn, pieces of fish or any other shellfish that happens to be to hand. Feed once a week with a piece the size of two peas.

Sickly specimens can be detected by a dwindling growth, and the hanging down of tentacles, together with a bedraggled and pallid appearance.

Since these animals are most successful in catching other marine creatures, it is wise to keep them in a small tank by themselves. They will catch small fish, prawns, small crabs with a regularity that soon depletes your stock. Since their tentacles are armed with a large number of stinging barbs they can quickly anaesthetise their victims, although they can be handled with complete immunity. Sensitive parts of the body, however, will quickly react to their poison barbs, as I discovered on one occasion. I had been siphoning the tank and the tentacles of an opelet anemone had become 'sucked-in' at the tank end. About twenty minutes later, wanting to make sure that all water was gone from the tube, I blew down it, my usual practice. The feel of that pipe was like a red-hot iron searing the lips and the pain lasted for a couple of hours—so beware when siphoning.

BEADLET ANEMONES (*Actinia equina*). These anemones are found much higher up the shore than others, and are common on the bare rocks at about half-tide level. They endure the scorching sun of a summer day and seem immune from its effect, although they often seek protection in some small crevice. They are very attractive in an aquarium because they remain open for long periods, and even after feeding their tentacles open rapidly. Their brownish colour shows well against white limestone rocks, but tends to become somewhat obscure when attached to red sandstone. Green and dark-red varieties can also be collected. An unusual spotted one is found on most shores and sometimes referred to as the strawberry anemone.

PARASITIC ANEMONES (*Calliactis parasitica*). Commonly found on the shells of whelks inhabited by hermit crabs (Fig 18). This is its normal home and in consequence it thrives under these conditions. Since the hermit is also a great predator and scavenger and will be well avoided by weaker creatures, many problems are overcome if the two are kept in one tank. If, however, you choose to collect the anemones alone, it is best done after a winter storm. Look amongst the weed along the tide-line and you may find some of them stranded, but little worse for their rough treatment.

Whether kept alone or with a hermit, they should be fed on pieces of mussel about twice a week.

Of all the anemones, these show the quickest reaction to any stimulus, and a touch will cause them to contract immediately, whilst they reopen again almost as soon. This sudden reaction is, no doubt, due in part to their natural moving habitat, for being carried about on the hermit they must have their moments of danger. Anyone who has watched hermit crabs moving over the rocks will have noticed how often they fall or somersault down the rocks, and if the anemone is to survive unharmed it needs to be able to contract suddenly.

Their feeding position on the whelk shell is usually near the sharp apex of the shell, and they bend over backwards to sweep the sea floor of all fragments, rather like an animated vacuum cleaner—and no doubt quickness of reaction helps them obtain food.

DAHLIA ANEMONES (*Tealia felina*). These are at one and the same time the most showy of all the anemones and the most—at times—disappointing. Showy because of their large tentacles and bulky size; disappointing because at times they remain closed for long periods, have a habit of dying off suddenly, and look rather ugly after feeding when their gut is extruded.

They can be collected by searching under rock ledges, for they shun the light and inhabit rock pools in the most inaccessible places. Wherever there is a ledge going 2ft under the rocks, and providing it is near the low-tide limit, there you will find the dahlia. Its grip of the rock is considerable and sometimes defeats all attempts to dislodge it without damage.

If placed in a tank with large pebbles, or even the larger fragments of sand, this anemone will attach pieces to its body until it is well sprinkled with them. One theory is that this is done for protection, but personal observation shows a different reason. The stones appear to camouflage the normal and rather obvious anemone body, and small crabs and prawns will walk right up the stones into the waiting tentacles, obviously unaware of any change in the normal 'feel' of the sea bed.

This species is another that will collect large quantities of evacuated food around its base, for it is a great feeder, and great diligence is needed to keep the basal area clear.

We have collected specimens of dahlia anemone as big across the disc as a tea plate, and one that size will consume a large prawn or small fish almost as soon as it catches one.

DAISY ANEMONES (*Cereus pedunculatus*). Rather elongated, but attractive anemones, sometimes found in rock pools where they insinuate their basal disc into deep fissures of the rock. In these places they are well-nigh impossible to collect, for damage invariably results. Fortunately they are often found in sand or mud where there are stones well below the surface and where the waters are sheltered and quiet. Collecting is easier at night, because the anemones can be easily spotted, and dug up with a fork or spade.

In spite of their natural love of deep 'burrowing', they thrive in an aquarium without deep sand, and their long extended bodies stretching upward resemble the curved trunks of palm trees in miniature.

Their food demands are meagre and a meal once a week will suffice.

The species mentioned in the foregoing pages are those that will be most commonly met, are easiest to keep and are attractive aquarium inmates. In the rocks tunnelled by burrowing shellfish down at the limit of low spring tide there live a fascinating variety of colourful anemones, fluorescent yellow, green and pink among them; but it takes patience and expertise to find them. For details of their habits and identification, consult a good reference book.

COMB-JELLIES (*Ctenophora*)

The comb-jellies (*Ctenophora*) (Fig 9) at first appear similar to jellyfish. They are fairly common inshore, especially during the late summer, and will be found well up river estuaries as well. They can be collected in a plankton net, or any small-mesh net such as can be made from muslin or curtain netting.

In an aquarium they are not long-lived, but their graceful swimming motion and two long trailing tentacles make them an attractive if temporary addition to the tank. Since the aquarist will probably be undertaking plankton hauls occasionally, he is bound to encounter them, and the safest way of transporting them home is in any clean glass jar in a small quantity of sea water.

Fig 9   Comb-jellies or sea gooseberries

WORMS (*Polychaeta*)

The number of species of worm is so great and their form so diverse, that only a few of the commoner ones will be described here.

RAGWORM (*Nereis diversicolor*). This worm is common in most muddy estuaries and shows preference for less salty water. Some portions of muddy shores are so covered with their holes that it would be impossible to place a saucer between them.

They can be collected by digging at random in the mud with a fork, and then breaking the mud down and sorting the worms from the other garbage that invariably collects in such places. As a matter of fact there is no occupation as messy as digging ragworm; you will need a good pair of rubber boots and a complete disregard for filthy mud all over your hands and clothes.

It is as food for other creatures that the aquarist will most want the ragworm. It is beloved of most species of fish. Small wrasse feed greedily on tiny pieces of cut worm, and those only 2in long will swallow a ragworm of the same length in one gulp. Tiny mullet can be persuaded to take fragments of crushed worm, but these must be small, for the mullet is a particular feeder. Pollack, bass, pouting, whiting, all the flat fish, gurnard and the rest, need no persuasion and thrive on this worm when it is fed to them once a week in winter or twice a week in summer.

To keep the worms alive simply make a box about 1ft square and 3in deep and line it with pitch in order to waterproof it. This box when thoroughly washed should be placed in a cool place with one side raised up about 1in: this can best be done by nailing a piece of 1in square timber along the bottom edge of one side. A small quantity of sea water is then placed in the box until it about half covers the bottom.

The worms are then put into the box where they will live quite well for a fortnight or more providing the place is cool.

Sometimes the worms are particularly active, and will

persistently crawl up the sides and out over the top of your box, to crawl away and die in some dark corner of the outhouse. To stop this, make a glass cover for the box. If the local glassworks can bore a few tiny airholes in the centre of your glass so much the better—or you can use a sheet of Perspex framed in wood and bore the holes yourself.

Nereis diversicolor can be kept in aquaria providing there is a sufficient depth of sand. A letter received from the well-known marine illustrator, the late L. R. Brightwell, FZS, may be of interest to those contemplating keeping this species. He found that they live well and burying into deep sand remain hidden throughout the day. At night they emerge from their burrows and feed on the half-mussel shells that he places in the tank for food. One worm can drag one of these shells below the sand and clear it completely in a matter of hours.

Nereis fucata is a rather more interesting species which is found in the whelk shell inhabited by the hermit crab *Eupagurus bernhardus*. A very high proportion of these shells contain the worm, so if you obtain a few crabs of this species try this:

Get your crab towards the front glass of the tank, and offer it a piece of mussel. As soon as it starts to feed keep a watch on the crab's right 'cheek'. If a ragworm is sharing its home, it will almost certainly crawl along this cheek and share the hermit's food. Although the sight of a worm taking mussel from the crab's jaw makes most women shriek, the crab seems perfectly happy about it all. On second thoughts perhaps 'happy' is not the right word, for frequently the crab will perform all sorts of queer manoeuvres to prevent the worm coming forward: the favourite is to squeeze itself as closely as possible towards the right side of the shell, or to give an abrupt jump upwards every time the worm's head appears out of the shell. In spite of this the worm is persistent and usually on the third or fourth attempt it thrusts forward and begins to feed.

One last word on ragworm; the large 'king' ragworm have big nippers that can give a painful bite, so when handling these take due care—'even a worm may turn'.

TUBEWORMS. Rather loosely perhaps, we are grouping together

all those worms that build, for their own protection, some form of tube. This tube can be of a mucilaginous nature as in the case of *Myxicola*, a rough muddy tube as used by *Sabella*, or a hard limestone tube as forms the home of certain tubeworms, such as the coiled tubeworm.

Sabella pavonina being one of the easiest to keep in an aquarium will be described first. This worm is found in certain muddy estuaries where the projecting sandy tubes resemble a forest of pencils sticking out a couple of inches above the surface of the mud. These tubes are normally about 1ft to 15in long, and when covered with water the worm extends a wide circle of brightly coloured tentacles that form a sort of small funnel. Each tentacle is armed with rows of minute hairs and these form a network designed to trap any food that passes in the current.

This brightly coloured funnel is in great contrast to the otherwise drab appearance of the tube, and this reason alone makes the worm a worthy aquarium inhabitant. If you cannot collect your own specimens they can be obtained from marine laboratories.

In your aquarium they must be kept apart from all predatory creatures, such as crabs and prawns, and are safest with comparatively sedentary creatures such as anemones. We have kept specimens for six months in small biscuit-tin tanks lit by a 20 watt bulb, and under such conditions they make good exhibits with a suitable rock background.

The tubes of this worm are not easy to arrange to the best possible advantage, for they are invariably twisted or curved towards the anterior end and in consequence will not 'sit prettily' on the sand. They are best held in place between small stones piled one on top of the other. Small quantities of excreta will settle on the sand below the disc of tentacles and these can be siphoned off, although the quantity is too small to foul the water.

Another very spectacular tubeworm is *Myxicola infundibulum*. Their funnel tentacles extend close above the top surface of the mud, but bury fairly deeply, and have to be dug out with a garden fork. Their first appearance is not exactly exciting for they are covered with mud and slime. If the slime is gripped reasonably firmly in one hand and then pulled through the fingers of the other hand it can be removed and the worm exposed. In this condition the worm is quite clean and can be carried in a jar of sea water. Soon after introduction to the aquarium the slime will again be secreted, but the light reddish-brown and purple-flecked funnel of tentacles makes a pretty sight.

In the same way as all fanworms they are filter feeders, and will thrive best when plentiful supplies of new sea water are available.

Another species is the sand mason (*Lanice conchilega*). This worm is usually found where sandy beaches give way to rocky formations or where small areas of sand lie between groups of rocks. The thin brittle tubes are clustered together until the whole colony resembles a rather untidy portion of honeycomb. Digging them out is no easy matter, for they bore deeply, but if you secure a few take them home and place them in an aquarium with plenty of fine sand so that they can continue to build their tubes.

They have longish reddish tentacles which are used both for the securing of detritus on which they feed, and for securing sand grains with which to build their tubes.

Finally, the worms that build their tubes of limestone. Perhaps the commonest of these are the coiled tubeworms, *Spirorbis spirillum* and *Spirorbis borealis*. The difference between the two species is that the former coils its tube anti-clockwise with the opening on the left, whereas the latter coils its tube clockwise with the opening facing right!

The tubes of these species are found commonly on the carapace of crabs and lobsters, covering stones, and often completely clothing a piece of seaweed such as wrack with their white coils.

They live well in aquaria, but need to be exhibited behind large magnifying glasses, for they are rather too small to be seen clearly without.

SEA MOUSE (*Aphrodite aculeata*). The most interesting of all marine worms, normally some 5in in length. It is often found on the shore after a storm has stirred it out of the mud in which it lives and thrown it up on the drift-line. At first glance its drab coloration gives no indication of its real beauty. Clean it off with a *soft* brush and place it in sea water, and immediately the hairs that clothe the sides of its body glow like rainbows. Why nature gives an animal that lives in mud so much beauty to obscure is indeed a mystery.

In aquaria it seldom thrives, for it needs a good bottom deposit from which to extract food. Attempts to feed a sea mouse with scraps of food are invariably doomed to failure, but if you chance upon a specimen it is worth keeping for a few days.

There are countless other species of worm that could be described. Some are common, but difficult to keep, and others rare and hardly likely to be encountered during a normal collecting trip. Perhaps an occasional reader will decide to specialise for a while in some species, in which case the books mentioned at the end of this book may be found helpful.

8

THE INVERTEBRATES

Molluscs Gastropoda and Lamellibranchia

This is a *phylum* of soft-bodied animals with shells. The shells can be external, as in the case of shellfish like cockles, or internal as in the case of the cuttlefish. They possess a foot which is variously adapted as a flat creeping sole or a swimming organ.

As will be known, the seashells we find on the beach are the late homes of animals. Some of these shells are in pairs and are known as bivalves and others are single or univalves. So numerous are the species that only the commonest will be mentioned here, and they can be kept alive in aquaria with varying degrees of success. Even within one species you will find that one animal will die whilst another survives quite happily. Some will live for months, then die unexpectedly. Univalves (Fig 10) such as the whelk (*Buccinum undatum*) can be recognised as 'sick' if they

Fig 10 Winkle (univalve) and mussel (bivalve)

cease to move around and usually adopt a position other than the normal. Bivalves (Fig 10) such as the mussel (*Mytilus edulis*) have a habit of dying quietly and giving no indication of their intention until it is too late, and your tank is polluted.

From all this you will gather that shellfish generally represent many problems in aquaria. With the minimum of experience you will soon discover which species are best suited to the conditions you have to offer, and the thing to do then is to specialise with these few and leave the rest. It is not anticipated that many aquarists will wish to reserve a tank solely for shellfish, for such a procedure is totally unnecessary. Most of them will live with a variety of other creatures.

Marine shells are infinitely more colourful than their freshwater counterparts and many are worthy of a place in the aquarium simply because of their outstanding colours. Their diets vary widely from carnivorous to herbivorous, whilst a few are quite omnivorous.

In the following pages a few of the common species are described, as these are the ones that beginners should try (Fig 11).

THE SOFT-BODIED ANIMALS—SHELLFISH

COMMON LIMPET (*Patella vulgata*). This is not an easy one to keep for any length of time, probably because too few aquarium tanks have a liberal growth of weed on the rocks. Limpets feed by browsing on the small green algae, and unless food is provided—and this is no easy matter—they will die of hunger in a clean tank. Their normal habit is to remain fixed in one spot on the rock and to make short journeys to browse before returning to their resting place. In an aquarium it is very difficult to provide ideal conditions.

THE DOG WHELK (*Nucella purpura lapillus*). The shell colour of this species varies from pure white through mauve and pink to black.

It is a carnivorous species that has a long lingual ribbon armed with sharp teeth. When feeding it bores a hole through the shell of its victim into its body. The lingual ribbon then continues to cut and tear and pass the food back to the whelk. It

Fig 11 Common shells: 1 limpets; 2 mussels; 3 dog whelks (dog winkles); 4 sting winkle; 5 flat periwinkles; 6 whelk; 7 painted top; 8 rednose cockle; 9 scallop

eats either barnacles or mussels: a black or mauve shell shows that the whelk has fed on mussels, whilst the white shell denotes barnacles. Sometimes an area of barnacles is cleared by the dog whelks, and so they begin to feed on mussels. This causes a colour change in their shells, which gives a blanded appearance. Having exhausted the mussels, if the time lag has enabled the barnacles to get re-established, they return to these.

In aquaria they are hardy and easy to feed.

NETTED DOG WHELK (*Nassarius reticulatus*). These are found in muddy sand, often just below the surface, and in the aquarium make excellent tank cleaners, scavenging on all waste food and dead matter.

PAINTED TOP SHELL (*Calliostoma zizyphinum*). Another species that browses on the weeds, it is highly colourful and will spawn readily in tanks. In a well-lit tank the shells require occasional cleaning if the bright colours of the shells are to be displayed to full advantage, because they soon develop a growth of green algae.

THE REDNOSE COCKLE (*Cardium aculeatum*). This shell can be collected on some beaches after periods of storm when the surf has stranded them along the drift-line. They are handsome animals when healthy, with bright orange fringes to the mantle and a deep red foot. Being filter feeders and normal inhabitants of sand, they do not thrive in aquaria. Occasional specimens can be kept for as long as three months or more.

SCALLOP (*Pecten maximus*). Young scallops are not especially hardy in small aquaria, but they do make a good show, especially when their valves are open and the beautiful fringe, dotted with pearl-like spots, is exposed. These dots are eyes and are situated in two rows, twenty-five to forty of them, each with a focusing lens and retina and capable of detecting the approach of enemies. In addition they have a fringe of sensory tentacles which detect the touch of starfish—their chief predator in nature.

But it is when moving they are of most interest, for as Brightwell so rightly terms them, they are indeed 'flying saucers'. They swim by opening and shutting the valves and spurting through the water, covering as much as 3ft in one leap. Then they zig-zag back to the tank floor. Since they are filter feeders their food requirement is a plentiful supply of good water, and the reason for the death of most aquarium specimens is no doubt starvation.

It is pure waste of time to keep scallops in a tank where any species of crab, however small, are living. Small hermit crabs thoroughly enjoy getting to work on a 2in scallop.

THE FLAT PERIWINKLE (*Littorina littoralis*). These are the small vari-coloured shells that cover areas of the rocks where the wrack grows thickest. Move a few fronds and you will find their yellow, red, green and black forms by the dozen.

They live quite well in aquaria, the chief trouble being their persistence in climbing right up to the top of the tank where they can no longer be seen. If you are prepared to keep returning them, then they are worth including. Their diet is vegetarian.

THE MUSSEL (*Mytilus edulis*). Too well known to demand description, this shellfish makes a useful addition to any tank solely for its filtering ability. It has been estimated that one fully-grown mussel can filter up to 10 gallons of water per day. Having seen the results of their work we have no doubt that such a figure is true.

Soon after introduction to the tank they will attach themselves to a rock or the sand by means of the byssus threads, and there will remain until you choose to move them forcibly. They have a habit of collecting a great deal of silt around their shells so it is good policy to siphon this area regularly. A healthy, feeding mussel should show a shell open about ⅛in with rows of gills a good dull yellow and deep red. A gaping shell usually means the mussel is dead or dying.

They do not require feeding, and will take their nourishment from the waste products of the fish and other occupants of your tank.

If mussels are kept for too long in a small tank, they filter out all the suspended matter and will then eventually die of starvation. Keep them, therefore, for not longer than two weeks at a time and then return them to their place on the shore.

Mussels can be used as a 'living filter' to clear water that has gone very cloudy. Place about thirty large mussels in a medium size jam jar and put this on the sandy bottom of the tank. Leave overnight and by morning the water will be perfectly clear. Then the jar must be very carefully and slowly drawn out of the tank to prevent the loose silt going back into the water.

If you wish to keep a quantity alive as a food, it is best done by placing them in a shallow earthenware dish that has a very small amount of sea water in the bottom. Cover the top with a sheet of glass to preserve a moist atmosphere, place in a cold position and they will live for days, until required.

QUEEN SCALLOPS (*Chlamys opercularis*). Filter feeders with an attractive array of shell colours, queens will occasionally swim around in the aquarium. Seldom found on the shore, they can sometimes be obtained from trawlermen.

STING WINKLE (*Ocenebra erinacea*). The beautifully carved shell of this animal makes a shapely addition to any tank, especially as they are reasonably hardy. They can be collected by searching among the low-tide rocks, where they will be found under the rock ledges and occasionally among the wracks. They are carnivorous and feed, in nature, on oysters, although other shellfish are equally relished.

THE WHELK (*Buccinum undatum*). This is an unpredictable species to keep in captivity, but experience has shown that providing a specimen survives the first two days in captivity it normally remains in good health for a considerable time.

Specimens can be collected from crabbers, or in deeper water some distance out from the shore they can be collected in a drop net baited with fish.

Before introducing them into your tank place them in a dish of sea water so that the slime they exude remains outside the tank, or the ensuing filth on the glass of the aquarium will look most unsightly. In captivity they can be fed on pieces of mussel, and in large tanks they will scavenge around and fend for themselves.

Signs of sickness can be detected by the whelk lying on its side with the large foot extended. If, when touched with the finger, the foot remains extended, it is almost certain the animal is dying.

THE CUTTLEFISH (*Sepia officinalis*). Few animals can rival these

Page 85 (*above*) A school of bass make attractive aquarium inhabitants, as they tend to swim in mid-water; (*below*) John Dory, an exotically shaped fish that makes a beautiful exhibit

Page 86 (*above*) A party of school children exploring pools on a rocky shore; (*below*) a common starfish

for interest, and they will live fairly successfully in a 4ft tank. Their habits are fascinating and there is always something new to observe as they display to each other or feed.

These strange animals are really shellfish, but instead of an external shell they possess an internal one. It is this that one picks up on the shore after a storm, and the same that is fed to cage birds (Fig 12).

During the months of May and June they will be found in inshore waters. They are not easily caught by aquarists, so the best method is to ask a crabber or trawlerman to get one for you.

For sheer interest nothing beats them, and their behaviour in an aquarium is the source of never-ending wonder. Cuttlefish sometimes refuse to adapt themselves to captivity, and on introduction to the tank will sulk in the darkest corner. There is only one thing that can be done in such circumstances, and that is to introduce another specimen. This in turn brings its difficulties: they usually fight. Having observed cuttlefish in the sea, it is obvious that the belligerent attitude results from the confined quarters, for in the sea they usually live amicably together.

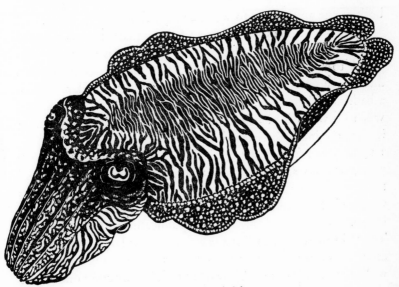

Fig 12 Cuttlefish

When in captivity they show remarkable colour changes, going from pure white to a vivid black and white zebra-like coloration in a matter of five seconds. When displaying before the opposite sex, or preparing for a fight, cuttlefish will extend their tentacles. A green phosphorescence spreads downwards across the face and over the tops of the eyes, whilst a shimmering wave of colour passes to and fro across the back. During daylight their eyes are mere slits shaped like two flat W's, but at night they open to their fullest extent.

Their choice of food is unpredictable, but large prawns are appreciated, and sometimes small strips of mackerel or tiny pollack and other fish. Give them alive. When feeding, the cuttlefish changes colour to a grey-white and approaches the prey very steadily and stealthily with only the slightest movement of the side fins. When within range of its prey the cuttle looks as if it is taking sights down its tentacles, which are extended forward and to a point directed towards the prey. Suddenly the two long retractable tentacles, kept within the facial disc, are shot outwards and dozens of sucker-pads attach themselves to the prey, as it is drawn back into the mouth. Here the parrot-like beak of the animal sets to work and the food is soon eaten.

Their one misdemeanour in so far as aquarists are concerned is their proneness to discharge their ink. This is normally supposed to be a defensive measure, but in aquaria it is often discharged at night and the following morning the tank resembles a bathful of black ink. Thus cuttlefish should only be collected when sea water is plentiful, for there is no easy way of cleaning it once the ink is discharged.

THE OCTOPUS (*Octopus vulgaris* and *Moschites cirrosa*). In some years, octopuses are fairly abundant, a few odd specimens find their way into the rocks around the beaches. This creature is surrounded with an aura of fantasy started probably by Victor Hugo, and fostered in various publications that deal with 'terror in the deep'. In fact the animal is not large, and a specimen measuring 3ft across the tentacles is about the largest you will encounter (Fig 13). Apart from luck in collecting one on the rocks or around pier piles, the best source of supply are crabbers:

Fig 13 Octopus

as the octopus invades their pots and eats the crabs, they are only too willing to get rid of them.

In captivity the octopus likes a cave or rock ledge to hide under, for in the sea it dwells in such places, and lying in wait for unsuspecting food to walk past its den. When some unfortunate crab does so, then out shoots the long tentacle and it is dragged into the enveloping wall of the remaining seven sucker-clad tentacles. If you do not provide a cave or hiding place, the octopus will chase around the tank collecting pieces of shell and stones, and by dragging them back into one corner of the tank, will build a small wall to hide behind. The tank should be securely covered, for these creatures have a habit of trying to get out, and the sight of an octopus crawling across the floor is not a happy one. Only the smallest specimens, less than 8in across the tentacles, should be kept in small tanks. They are unpredictable and exceedingly difficult to keep without plenty of water and a good circulation.

Their favourite food is small crabs, which should be kept in the tank with them, to be eaten as required.

SEA SLUGS. Unlike their counterparts on land, these creatures are colourful and quite attractive in appearance.

The sea lemon (*Archidoris britannica*) is one of the commonest, and will be found under rock ledges from April onwards. Its food consists of sponges, and these can be collected from the same rocks; wherever you find the slug, there will be sponges nearby.

During the late spring it will readily lay its eggs in your aquarium, and the egg ribbon is a delicate structure well worthy of a place.

In certain localities each year, enormous numbers of sea hare (*Aplysia punctata*) come ashore to spawn. They can be kept with varying degrees of success, but are definitely not hardy in small tanks with limited circulation of fresh sea water. Their food in captivity is sea lettuce, and this can be introduced freshly by collecting it from the shore pools.

One other fairly common slug is the grey sea slug (*Aeolida papillosa*). Its food is sea anemones, and its resemblance to one is quite extraordinary. In small aquaria it does not thrive, but it will live for a couple of months and can then be returned to the sea to recover.

In the course of normal collecting you will doubtless encounter various other species of sea slug, many shapely and of quite beautiful colours. Here lies a rich field of research for the aquarist willing to discover the secret of success in keeping them alive and healthy for long periods.

THE SPINY-SKINNED ANIMALS (*Echinodermata*)

STARFISH (*Asteroidea*). Few sea creatures have developed into such popular animals as the starfish. One sees it on most of the summertime advertisements, and it has its place on the cover of numerous seashore books. The uninitiated must imagine that the shores of this country teem with starfish—yet, in fact, on many of our beaches one has to search for many weeks to find a single specimen (Fig 14).

Starfish have five or more arms, covered on their underside with hundreds of tiny tube feet. These are used as a means of progression from place to place, but primarily as a means of holding fast to rock surfaces and for feeding. They can regrow a damaged arm, and a brittlestar in an aquarium can grow an extra 5cm on an arm in less than two months. In small aquaria it is best to keep only perfect specimens, as the discharge from any injury on a starfish spreads through the water, and can turn it white.

The commonest source of supply is the crabber, for starfish will enter crab pots and feed on the bait. Sunstars, brittlestars and common starfish can all be obtained in this way. Low-tide rock pools and rock ledges are the best areas to search when collecting yourself.

BRITTLESTAR (*Ophiocomina nigra*). This black animal is a most attractive specimen and is comparatively active. It can move with great rapidity when food is introduced into the tank. In a small 2ft tank you can keep up to a dozen large black brittlestars. To feed them use pieces of mussel flesh, and whilst this can be

Fig 14 Common starfish: 1 sunstar; 2 brittlestar; 3 spiny starfish;
4 common starfish; 5 starlet

dropped in haphazardly, and the animals left to find it, it is far better to feed them individually. This can be done by placing the piece of food on the tips of their arms. As soon as food contacts the arm they seize it with a twisting motion, and within a few seconds that food has passed down the arm and is placed in the mouth. Healthy brittlestars can catch live food such as mysis or small prawns. They tend to congregate in groups in your tank, and if a piece of food is dropped amongst them there is invariably a wild scramble of threshing arms as they all endeavour to eat what is offered.

As their name implies they have extremely brittle limbs, and these are easily broken, so extreme care is needed when handling them (Fig 14).

For a beginner, this animal is a good one, for it will live peaceably with almost anything, and can be a good scavenger providing the particles are large enough. In colonies on the sea bed they have been known to spread for up to two miles in densely packed masses.

The small brittlestar (*Ophiothrix fragilis*) is far less hardy. It is a creature that relishes a good bottom deposit and the clean floor of a good aquarium does not provide the correct habitat. Also it tends to crawl away and hide under rocks, and is therefore best kept in aquaria where the rocks are cemented in place.

SUNSTAR (*Solaster papposus*). The most colourful of the starfish, its beautiful patterned body makes a wonderful attraction to any aquarium tank. It tends to spend most of its time on the sides and glass of the tank, where it can be fed, with patience on the aquarist's part. Use a glass rod and secure the piece of mussel flesh to the end of it. With the tip of your finger gently prise the animal free from its attachment on one side of its body, allowing it to continue gripping with the remaining arms. The glass rod with the food should then be placed so that the food is released into the centre of the disc, and the animal is left to feed. Whilst this sounds a long and tedious method of feeding a sea creature, it is nevertheless necessary.

Sunstars have a habit of dying without warning, and if you notice that one of your specimens is lying rather flatly on the floor of the tank, without any movement, the chances are it would be safer to move it at once.

Most handsome of the sunstars is *Solaster papposus*, which has as many as thirteen arms, this number being variable. Specimens up to 2in across keep well in small tanks, but any over that size are very difficult.

THE STARLET (*Asterina gibbosa*). The smallest starfish the aquarist is likely to encounter on the seashore is the starlet (*Asterina gibbosa*). This little animal seldom exceeds 4cm across the disc and is of a dull khaki coloration. Its favourite haunt is under rock ledges, or on the under-surface of sizeable stones towards low-tide limit. In small 2ft tanks it lives well, but is singularly inactive and will remain in one place for as long as a week at a time. It looks quite attractive, for when on the back of the tank its shape is pleasing.

COMMON STARFISH (*Asterias rubens*). This species is very variable in colour, ranging from pale red to dark mauve and also orange. Its natural food consists of shellfish, and for many years this starfish has been regarded as a serious pest of the oyster beds. Work by D. A. Hancock (Fisheries Laboratory, Burnham-on-Crouch) has thrown light on their feeding habits. The following quotation is taken from the *Journal* of the Marine Biological Association UK:

> *Asterias rubens* is found most likely to be associated with large numbers of *Crepidula* (Slipper Limpet), the most serious competitor of the oyster. Laboratory experiments showed that although *Asterias* occasionally ate spat and adult oysters, the greater part of its food was made up of organisms which are competitors of the oyster. The smaller sizes of *Asterias* ate large numbers of barnacles, with occasional spat or oysters and *Crepidula*.

So slipper limpets would provide good food for aquarium specimens.

Asterias must be watched closely in tanks. The first signs of a decline in health can be detected by the starfish throwing off an arm. Within twenty-four hours of this it will be dead and the water fouled. Providing the correct food, slipper limpets for large specimens and barnacles for the smaller ones, will avoid much trouble.

PURPLE-TIPPED SEA URCHIN (*Psammechinus miliaris*). Everywhere around Britain's west coast this species will be seen attached to rock ledges and under weed. Its habit is to crawl around with numerous small stones and shells attached to its spines. In an aquarium tank it soon collects a dozen or more items and moves around looking like a walking rubbish heap (Fig 15).

Fig 15 Sea urchins: (*top*) edible urchin; (*left*) purple-tipped urchin; (*bottom*) heart urchin

When collecting, keep these sea urchins in a separate container, for they very soon collect other species on their spines. Sea anemones, even, will get firmly stuck, and often one damages them when trying to release them from the urchin.

In the aquarium tank they are not a very active species, and should be fed on scraps of mussel, although they often spend hours on the bottom browsing on algae and scraps left from the other inhabitants of the tank.

THE EDIBLE SEA URCHIN (*Echinus esculentus*). This is a much larger animal, and in the breeding season is a vivid purple colour (Fig 15). A healthy specimen always has long tentacles extended and these are waved about on the ceaseless search for food and 'foothold'. Compared with the previous species, this one is active, for it is always moving around on the sides of the tank, and can be fed on small pieces of fish, mussel, etc. On one occasion a specimen 3in across was seen feeding on a piece of throng weed that was placed in the tank for temporary decoration. They also browse on algae.

A common source of supply is the crab boat, but wherever your specimens come from, examine each one carefully before introducing it into the tank. Damaged specimens can quickly be detected by a discoloration of the shell, which usually goes brown and then black. These colours appear in patches and the spines invariably drop off in the area, and since there is no cure for the internal damage that has been done it is best to release the creature back into the sea. Although possessing a fairly strong outer covering their internal organisation is exceptionally fragile, and only extreme care in handling and transporting will ensure a good specimen for your tank.

An unpleasant trade has developed in the collection, killing and drying of these urchins, so that they can be sold fitted up with an electric bulb as decorative lamps. Perhaps as more people become involved with and aware of the fascination of creatures in the sea, enough understanding will develop for us all to want to enjoy their living beauty rather than their dead remains.

9

THE INVERTEBRATES

Crustacea

Included under this heading are the vast number of crabs, lobsters, shrimps, prawns and barnacles, down to the ever-abundant sand-hopper.

Broadly speaking these animals are easy to keep providing due consideration is given to their size. Since many of them are actively predaceous and carnivorous you will be inviting trouble if you endeavour to keep too many of them together, or place them with less protected animals. Given plenty of space they are quite hardy.

As a *phylum*, they have been the most successful of all animals, and their numbers greatly exceed those of all other animals put together. This success is in part due to their hard outer skeleton, made of a substance called chitin; because of its firmness arthropods are able to support their body in the absence of water, and so exist on land.

A brief glance at a crab will reveal a number of appendages. Originally they were mostly used for movement from one place to another, but as the centuries passed certain of these appendages became more specialised for other work. Thus a crab has two large nippers as a means of attack and defence. Its eyes are compound, which is to say that instead of having a single lens as we have, it has dozens of smaller lenses all fused into one eye. One disadvantage of this is that the image received by the animal must be of poor quality, and resemble a series of dotted pictures. We recall seeing a photograph taken through the eye of an insect and the head of the 'sitter' was repeated once for each eye.

THE LOBSTER (*Homarus vulgaris*)

Taking the lobster as a specific example, its cuticle of chitin is made hard by a mixture of calcium salts obtained from the sea. It has two pairs of antennae which are used in the quest for food, detection of prey and enemies and similar work (Fig 16). The mouth-parts are complicated, but in essence consist of jaws to crush the food, maxillas which pass the food into the mouth and another maxilla which is used in the breathing system. Then there are three pairs of maxillipeds, whose chief function is to deal with the food, break it up ready for the mouth to eat.

If the aquarist looks closely at any large lobster, he will notice that the two large nipper claws are not of equal size or shape. The larger one has well-rounded 'spikes': this is used for crushing, and anyone who has seen a large lobster seize a stick will appreciate the enormous muscular power it possesses. It can squeeze an ordinary broomstick until the wood creaks and cracks, so it can be imagined what will happen to the finger of any unfortunate who mishandles a lobster. The smaller nipper has sharp spines on it and this one is used for seizing and breaking up its prey. A hungry lobster will attack anything and is a very great forager. In addition to having jaws and specialised parts for crushing food, this animal also possesses a gizzard which is further armed with muscularly controlled teeth.

The lobster has twenty pairs of gills. They are attached to the legs and lie underneath the carapace, or great shield, covering the forward end of the animal. Water from which the life-giving oxygen is extracted is drawn upwards through these gills and passed outwards by the shovelling action of the maxillas. This explains why when a lobster is offered some piece of food which it does not like it is able to 'blow' it forward with considerable force.

Now the lobster forages at night, and in consequence eyes are of little use to it. Evolution has given it an enormous number of

Fig 16 Edible crab and lobster

bristles all over the legs and antennae. They are numbered in thousands and are of two kinds, some sensitive to touch and others sensitive to chemicals. Thus the lobster is able to detect its food by touch and scent, a useful adaptation in a world of darkness where everything is on the prowl for food and speed is essential.

The sex of the lobster can be distinguished by looking for the external reproductive opening which lies between the bases of the third legs in the case of the female and between the fifth pair in the case of males. When mating the male releases its sperm close to the females and the eggs are fertilised as they emerge. The eggs are then attached to the swimmerettes of the female by a sticky secretion, and in this state a female lobster is referred to as being 'berried'.

KEEPING LOBSTERS IN AQUARIA. Few aquarists will be so fortunate as to obtain 1in lobsters, and the average size will probably be nearer 6in in body length, with nippers making another 3in. Lobsters this size can be kept in a 4ft tank quite comfortably and are very attractive exhibits, providing they are taken out about once a month and the carapace and segments brushed with a stiff brush to remove the dirt that collects there. This cleaning operation restores the bright blue body colour and is well worth doing.

When handling your lobster always approach from behind. Let the hand rest low along its back and grip the animal with thumb and forefinger just behind the two large nippers. The lobster will wave its nippers most menacingly, but cannot touch you providing you keep your hand and wrist sloping backwards. Frequently when your hand draws close to the animal it will turn, or attempt to turn, so the more smoothly and quickly you perform the operation the better it will be for your nerves.

Lobsters can be collected from inshore rocks although in such places they are not abundant. Look under weed-hung ledges and in crevices. A much less troublesome way is to ask a crab fisherman to get you one.

Feeding is simple. Give a piece of gurnard or other fish about the size of a packet-book of matches twice to three times a week. After feeding take a careful look around your tank to ensure that all scraps have been eaten. Although a nocturnal feeder, once acclimatised to the lighted aquarium most lobsters will feed under your electric lamp. Those that do not can be fed just before you put the lights out, so that they have the rest of the dark hours to help themselves.

Very shallow caves are ideal in a lobster tank, for then the animal can back into them and be well content whilst still being in full view of the aquarist. Deep caves are useless if you want to see your inmates.

A lobster's hard chitinous skin cannot grow, and as with all crabs and prawns, at intervals depending upon growth, feeding and general health, this skin splits along the centre line of the carapace and the lobster emerges from its old skin. When moulting, as this process is termed, antennae, legs and every part is withdrawn from the inside of the old skin. It is an amazing process to watch, and the old skin makes an extra exhibit to have beside the tank. A series can be kept recording the growth of the particular lobster.

CRABS

In the main their life takes much the same pattern as that of the lobster, except that small crabs, such as green shore crabs and swimming crabs, are much more predaceous and will attack almost anything when hungry. For pandemonium let loose, little can rival feeding time in an aquarium tank holding an assortment of crabs. One crab obtains a piece of food, a second does likewise. Immediately the first crab attacks the second to try to rob it of its food, regardless of the fact that probably the piece it already has is twice the size of the other fragment.

THE GREEN SHORE CRAB (*Carcinius maenas*). The green shore crab is found everywhere in rock pools or comes up in vast numbers in prawn pots. It is a quick, darting, pugnacious and belligerent crab, resting for only short periods between foraging expeditions. Always keep these apart from all other delicate and unprotected animals, for even a tiny, one-penny-sized crab will attack and devour a sea urchin the size of a cherry.

A proportion of shore crabs will be found to have an egg-like mass attached to the under side of the abdomen. This is the body of a parasite, *Sacculina carcini*, which has ramifying rootlets growing throughout the body of the crab, and thus obtains its food at the expense of the host. This parasite was once a kind of barnacle and through aeons of time it settled on the backs of crabs and slowly developed into a parasite. Because of its presence the host never moults, and in consequence the shell will usually be found to be liberally covered with a multitude of barnacles, tubeworms and the like. Nor can the crab reproduce. Ultimately the parasite dies and the crab can then resume its normal growth and reproduction.

As with all crabs, food is an easy problem, for it will consume practically everything that is offered, and a small one in the tank is a useful scavenger.

THE VELVET SWIMMING CRAB (*Portunus puber*). This is a species whose legs are adapted for swimming by being quite flattened and provided with a fringe of swimming hairs like the blade of an oar. In pursuit of small pollack or other swimming prey they can move at an alarming speed, and they are experts in climbing out of tanks. Always have a cover on the tank when keeping them, for once out of the tank they will hide up and die.

THE SPIDER CRAB (*Hyas araneus*). This crab is both quaint and fascinating. Its great ungainly long legs move slowly to give it the appearance of an automaton (Fig 17). Its spiked back is frequently covered with a thick growth of hydroids and small algae, some of which are placed there by the crab as camouflage material. When introduced to a new tank the crab will pick up any loose weed if it is provided and place it slowly but surely all over its back.

Spider crabs, edible crabs and lobsters can be kept together, providing they are kept well fed. There will be occasional sparring between the spiders and the lobsters, but the edible crabs remain aloof. We have never seen a fight that ended in disaster, although we have often seen a spider being 'taken for a ride' on the back of a lobster. The ensuing struggle is laughable because one is certain that no damage is done, or perhaps even intended.

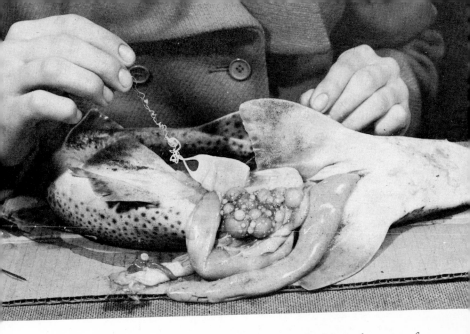

Page 103 (above) Removing the egg capsule from a dogfish; in the centre of the picture can be seen the developing eggs in the ovary; (below) baby dogfish in the artificial egg capsule described in the text; this one is about seven months old

Page 104 (*left*) The author and his partner Ron Peggs filming a cine sequence for a BBC natural history film; (*below*) a useful lighting rig for aquarium photography

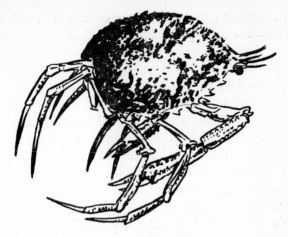

Fig 17 Spider crab

Spider crabs are not easy to acclimatise to aquarium tanks, but once settled down they will live for a long time, if fed on pieces of gurnard or white fish. The shell can be scrubbed periodically to remove the dirt that collects amongst the spikes. These crabs in particular are a menace where there are any loose airlines and diffusers placed in the centre of the tank, or any other areas where it can get tangled up. Its legs will certainly find that airline, so keep the air supply tight up in one corner.

Crabs and lobsters are in constant danger of losing one of their large nippers, either through direct attack from other crabs or by getting it crushed under a large stone. The action of casting a leg is carried out this way. If, for instance, the leg is pinned under a rock, certain muscles come into action which bend the leg to an extreme angle, so placing undue strain on a predesigned line, the breaking plane of the leg. The leg then snaps off, leaving a thin membrane covering the break; the blue blood quickly congeals and prevents further damage. As the crab moults the next time, a small stump of the new leg will appear. This stump slowly develops into another leg as each successive moult takes place, until ultimately there is no difference between the new leg and its original one.

THE EDIBLE CRAB (*Cancer pagurus*). This crab is a lethargic fellow (Fig 16), prone to seek the shelter of a corner, and there to crouch down with nippers folded across its face, remaining thus like some carved image of a real crab. On first introduction it will roam ceaselessly, but once settled there it remains, except to rise forward and smother the food as it drops.

We once had a tank with a hole in the bottom covered with a piece of quarter plate glass set in glazing compound. Through this glass a coloured light shone up through the air bubbles which came out of the diffuser, placed on this glass. One long-to-be-remembered morning, when the public was thronging the aquarium, there was a sudden gush of water and a stream shot out across the floor. The crab had managed to get his claw under the lip of the glass and had pulled it up, letting loose a flow of water.

Immediate repairs were undertaken and life returned to normal. Two hours later the sound again dripped through the aquarium, and again a stream of water issued forth. The crab this time was walking across the tank, grasping a piece of glass aloft as if defying all and sundry to stop him scuttling the tank and himself. From this you will gather that crabs occasionally awake from their comatose condition and have brief spells of troublesome activity.

Crabbers will often let you have an edible crab with an anemone on its back. On certain grounds where crabs are caught, plumose anemones are frequently found on their backs, and they make an unusual and interesting exhibit in the tank. After a time the anemone may leave the crab's back and attach itself to the rocks or floor of the tank.

THE HERMIT CRAB (*Eupagurus bernhardus*). Finally among crabs, the most interesting is the large hermit crab. For those not acquainted with the habits of this species the following description may prove of interest (Fig 18).

Soon after the young crabs leave the plankton and settle down on the bottom they seek a tiny shell, the vacated home of a shellfish, and settle down inside. They do this because nature has given them a very delicate and soft abdomen which would be

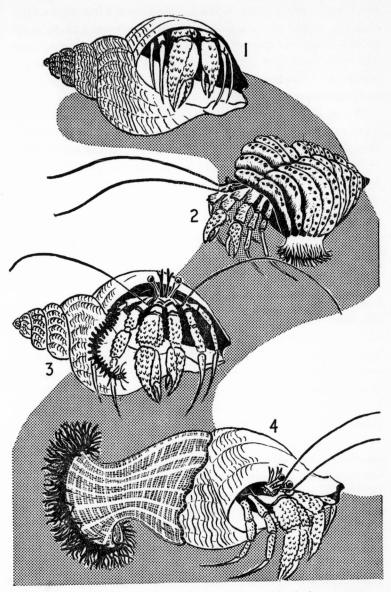

Fig 18 Hermit crabs: 1 curled up in shell; 2 with cloak anemone;
3 with ragworm; 4 with anemone living on shell

so attractive to predators that it has to be protected. Slowly the crab grows through a succession of moults in which the skins are cast, and as it grows the hermit seeks ever larger shells in which to place its body. House-hunting is a lifetime's job for hermit crabs, and even in an aquarium they must be provided with an assortment of shells should they wish to change.

When seeking larger premises the crab investigates each empty shell with extreme care. First the shell is examined with a brushing motion of the long antennae, and when satisfied the crab moves closer and begins to inspect the surface with its legs. The shell is eventually turned so that the opening is uppermost, and then the hermit inserts its small nipper followed by the larger one, and searches every twist and turn of the shell. This inspection is merely to ascertain that there is no living creature in the shell likely to attack when the crab inserts its abdomen in a moment. Finally satisfied, the crab moves its own shell into a strategic position alongside the new home. A careful and pro-longed survey of the surrounding water is then made, to make quite sure that no enemies are about, and with a sudden leaping twist its body curves out and over into the new shell. A moment-ary adjustment then occurs as it grips the columella by twisting its abdomen around it, and then the body is drawn in and out to drive out any air bubbles that may lurk inside the new home.

Sometime after this has happened, a ragworm arrives on the scene, drawn by some instinct we cannot explain, and it begins a survey of the hermit's new home. Slowly and with infinite stealth it crawls up the shell from the pointed end towards the opening from whence the crab's body extends. The worm intrudes its head into the space between the hermit and the shell, and in a sudden rush disappears inside the shell where it will now live until such time as the crab seeks another shell. Living in this way the worm has an easy time for, as we have seen, when the hermit secures a piece of food the ragworm crawls forward, extends its head from the right-hand space of the shell and shares the food with the crab.

That makes two creatures living together quite happily. Now a third animal joins the community. An anemone (*Calliactis parasitica*) attaches itself to the outside of the shell, or sometimes the crab actually places it there. This anemone settles down on the pointed end of the shell, and whenever the hermit and worm have had a meal and a few scraps have fallen on the sea bed the anemone bends over, and like a vacuum cleaner, sweeps up the scraps on its tentacles. They all live happily together in an old whelk shell.

Returning to keeping hermits in aquaria, providing a lively specimen is secured it settles down quickly and will feed the day after capture. The anemone can be fed separately with tiny pieces of mussel, because there will probably be insufficient food on the floor of your tank. Mussel appears to be hermits' favourite food, although they will accept a great variety of fish, and peeled uncooked prawn.

Providing they are put in a tank which has a good few rocks spread over the floor, their antics will amuse you for ever. A common accident that happens in your aquarium, but never in the sea, is caused by their crawling over the diffuser. The air rushes into the shell and makes it buoyant. The crab is floated to the surface where it remains suspended, and gropes for a non-existent foothold, upside down and very disturbed.

In the springtime most hermits will be 'berried', and such specimens are of further interest to keep because they can be observed flushing their eggs: the hermit extends its body from the shell and with a rolling motion the eggs are swayed about. When ready to spawn, the young are released from the egg, and the tiny zoea can be seen swimming upwards into the water from the body of the crab. These zoea will not live long in your aquarium, for food is difficult to provide.

Not easy to collect on the shore, but commonly taken by trawlers, is the hermit crab *Eupagurus prideauxi*. This one goes into a shell when it is tiny, and very soon after the cloak anemone (*Adamsia palliata*) comes and settles over the shell. As the hermit grows so does the anemone, and in consequence the hermit never seeks a larger shell, for its body is completely shrouded and protected by the anemone.

In all the rock pools will be found young hermit crabs in an amazing variety of shells, and a few of these in each tank make good scavengers, for their constant activity carries them over the entire bottom of your tank and ensures all scraps are cleared up.

One last remark about hermits. Their right claw is always much larger than the left and they are able to retreat into their shell and use this great claw as an effective barrier to any predators seeking a free meal.

THE PRAWN (*Leander serratus*)

Prawns (Fig 19) are easy to keep in well-aerated water that is kept fairly cool, and are very easy to collect with a hand net. Scrape your net under the rock ledges and along the weed curtains of rock pools, and in the deeper water beyond the edge of the rocks. Use a drop net at night baited with a fish skeleton.

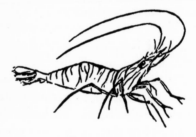

Fig 19 Prawn

It is not generally realised that prawns, besides being scavengers, are active predators on smaller fry. We have seen a 2in prawn swim into a shoal of small 1in pollack and catch one, actually killing and eating it. Their capacity for food is enormous, and they seem to be able to feed almost continuously. As with so many common animals they are neglected, due in part to the fact that folk imagine they are 'just prawns'. Put half a dozen in a small tank and study them and you will soon discover their habits are worth watching.

They are extremely clean animals and carry out regular toilet operations that last anything up to ten minutes at a time. Using their legs they will brush their bodies, inserting a leg into the space between swimmerettes and removing every speck of dirt that collects. The antennae are stroked and the body curved into a close letter C in order to clean the tail.

A few prawns should be kept in every tank if only for their scavenging habits; watch them when you feed less active animals, for they will catch dropping food before it reaches the sand.

Although with the onset of winter most prawns move offshore into deeper, warmer water, we have kept prawns in temperatures as low as 33° F for a week at a time, when other species have succumbed. In the spring and early summer they will be 'in berry', and carrying their eggs between their swimmerettes.

Pottering around rock pools will reveal a variety of prawn-like animals mostly quite small and in the ½in to 1in range. On an incoming summer tide large numbers of prawns can be watched swimming along the deepening gullies, or on an ebb-tide swimming back into deeper water.

THE SHRIMP (*Crangon vulgaris*)

These are not seen easily during the hours of daylight because they burrow beneath the sand and are thus camouflaged from human eyes. They can be collected by pushing a shrimp net over sand below the limit of low tide, or in pools where sand covers the bottom.

In appearance they are not unlike a prawn, but lack the jagged projecting rostrum and their body is much more flattened, with the head ending more squared (Fig 20).

If keeping them in aquaria it is best to have practically no sand at all, or otherwise they will always be hidden from view. Practically nothing edible comes amiss to shrimps. As they feed on all manner of green stuff and animal matter, feeding presents no problems.

Their burrowing habit is worth watching: they shuffle about with their legs extended forward and back, and sweep the sand aside with rapidly moving swimmerettes. Finally, when a deep

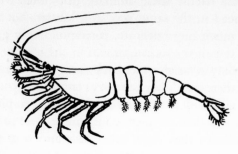

Fig 20 Shrimp

enough excavation is made, they use their long antennae to push sand over their backs, thus completing a very effective camouflage.

NORWAY LOBSTER (*Nephrops norvegicus*)

The Norway lobster is an attractive creature if you can obtain a few specimens. Its pastel-shaded body is in complete contrast to that of practically every other sea creature, and although it tends to remain stationary, it has reasonably active times. With its long front nippers it will make the most threatening attempts to seize any prawn or fish that comes too close—but it never succeeds. In fact all this appears to be more a defensive than an offensive attitude (Fig 21).

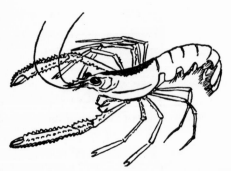

Fig 21 Norway lobster

If you must handle these animals, grip them very gently behind the head in the same way as a lobster, but since their shell is very much more delicate, correspondingly greater care is necessary. If you try to catch them in the confined space of an aquarium they invariably race backwards with extraordinarily rapid flips of their tails. They can move faster than your hand, so are better caught with a small net. The system is to place the net behind them and then to insert your finger close to their face, with the result that they shoot backwards into your net.

In captivity they feed on mussel, pieces of prawn, small cubes of white fish or tiny ragworms.

BARNACLES (*Balanus balanoides*)

By no means least in interest among the crustaceans is the common barnacle. The young ones which swim free in the sea are typical crustaceans, even though the adult form hardly resembles one. This is primarily because they have settled to a sedentary life and cemented themselves to a rock.

Since they live on the most exposed surfaces, receiving the fiercest buffetings of surf and sea-hurled rocks, they need to have a stout shell. They are filter feeders, and it is perhaps this one fact that makes them interesting animals to keep in aquaria. They literally kick their food into their mouths. If one is placed

Fig 22 Barnacles feeding

in a small tumbler of sea water and left quietly for a matter of minutes, it will come to life. The foot can be seen rhythmically 'grasping' through the water and extracting anything edible that happens to be there (Fig 22). We have kept these animals for long periods without any losses, for they are most adaptable and hardy. If the water is filtered or left unchanged too long they become quiescent, but if only a jarful of new sea water is added to the tank they begin to feed almost at once.

Never try to chip the barnacles off the rocks. Look for a group on the edge of a rock and then with a hammer and cold chisel remove a portion of the rock. This will ensure no damage is done. In an aquarium they should be placed close to the front glass so that they can be seen feeding. If a magnifying glass is fixed in front of the tank, the feeding apparatus can be seen at work.

SQUAT LOBSTERS

All around the shores you will find the small green squat lobster (*Galathea squamifera*). If a stone is turned over on damp muddy sand, near low-tide mark, you will certainly see the rattling retreat of one of these animals, as with rapid thrusts of its tail it makes for new cover. In size they average about ½in (Fig 23).

In aquaria they tend to hide under any small shell or stone

Fig 23 Squat lobster

that is available, and in consequence do not make really suitable inmates unless you can arrange to have no available cover. Even then, they still seek the darkest corner of the tank and remain almost invisible.

As far as feeding goes it is best to let them scavenge on what has been left by other occupants of your tank.

If you can contact a trawlerman or crabber you will be able to secure a specimen of the larger squat lobster (*Galathea strigosa*). This species is brilliantly banded with blue on a red body and makes an almost tropical addition to your collection. It is not too easy to encourage to feed, but from the appearance of the great nippers one would imagine it would seize anything and tear it to shreds.

When the water cools down to below 40° F they become lethargic and will soon die unless the water can be warmed up a few degrees.

They can seldom be collected in rock pools, and their occurrence in deeper water is just as unpredictable. For instance, we have known crabbers catch a few dozen in a week and then go for a month and not see another one.

THE CRAWFISH (*Palinurus vulgaris*)

This handsome animal does make very rare appearances in inshore regions, but the best chance of getting a specimen is to ask a crab fisherman (Fig 24).

It has an orange-brown body richly speckled with deep red and a wicked armament of jagged spines along the lower sides of the abdomen. Great care is needed when picking one up, for it will flip its tail violently and unless you handle it correctly you will get a sorely damaged hand. Since, in captivity, they are restless animals they need a fairly large tank; 4ft is the minimum, unless the specimen is a particularly small one.

Crawfish lack the great nippers of the lobster, but feed on pieces of white fish readily. To keep them occupied, place a large mussel in the tank and invariably they will spend a long time getting it open and devouring the contents.

Fig 24 Crawfish

Amongst the crustaceans not mentioned in the foregoing pages there are innumerable species that can be kept in marine aquaria. These include such animals as the common and ubiquitous *Gammarus* and *Orchestia*. These are the sand-hoppers that cluster under drying weed on the drift-line and jump frenziedly whenever a piece is lifted.

Many other forms of crustaceans are too small to warrant mention as aquarium assets, but those who intend to keep them should refer to one of the many books that deal with these animals, some of which are mentioned at the end of this book.

10

THE VERTEBRATES

Fish

It is a common but erroneous belief that marine fish are difficult to keep in aquaria. Naturally there is a definite size limit both for the fish and the tank and naturally the sizes of the two are closely related.

When we speak of size we do not refer solely to length, although this is the common way of referring to fish. We refer in fact to overall size plus weight. For instance, a bass 12in long is in no way as large as a plaice of the same length, and whilst the former could be kept in a 4ft tank, the latter could not.

Broadly speaking if you want to go in for marine fish of over 4oz in weight you will need a 4ft tank. As an illustration of what can be kept in a 4ft tank, 2ft wide by 2ft deep, we give the following groups that have lived successfully for a long time:

Three wrasse (*Labridae*) approximately 9in in length.
One bass (*Serranidae*) 1ft in length.
One topknot (*Bothidae*) (a flatfish) 5in in length.
Five pouting (*Gadidae*) approximately 6in in length.
One pollack (*Gadidae*) 9in in length.

In marine tanks the rule of 1in of fish to a gallon of water can be disregarded, for much more attention has to be paid to the nature of the fish, eg whether they are active or quiet.

To give advice as to what one can keep is a more difficult problem than one would imagine, for it is really a question of getting to know the fish. And perhaps that is the marine aquarist's first and foremost task. In the following pages we give the results of our own experience, but after keeping fish for many years we have learned that not only has each species its own peculiarities, but individuals within the species differ to a greater extent than is commonly imagined.

We had some young wrasse once, 2in fellows, five of them being introduced on the same day. Right from the start one of them remained active and swam about in mid-water whilst the remainder took up positions around the rocks. They all lived happily and fed well, but the four never summoned up the necessary courage to swim about. Or perhaps the swimmer was the one exception to the normal wrasse behaviour.

All marine fish resent disturbance of any sort. Bumps on the floor transmitted to the water frighten them, tapping the glass does the same, but most of all they are scared by the aquarist's head or hand appearing over the surface of the tank. If you must look in the top, or put your hand or net in, then do it quietly. Never give a sudden movement when trying to catch a fish in the tank for it can move faster than you, and the panic it creates spreads to every fish in the tank. The usual result of such excitement is a series of hurtling bodies hitting the floor—and the loss of some good stock.

We have often read that lighting arrangements should be controlled so that no lights flash on suddenly. In our experience this makes no difference at all, and we once set out to test the effect of sudden switching on and off. The fish continued to swim as steadily as they had all along. If you switch on the lights of a wrasse tank after dark you will find the occupants asleep on ledges, and apart from a swivelling eye directed upwards, no other notice is taken.

Sea fish are extremely sensitive to sudden temperature changes. They cannot endure a sudden drop, for instance, of five degrees, but if the same drop takes seven days there will be no ill effects.

Although the matter of feeding is discussed in the next chapter, it is so important that we shall emphasise it once more. Marine fish should be fed twice a week in winter and never more than three times a week in summer. Overfeeding merely encourages disorders, both in the health of the fish and in the condition of the tank.

CATCHING AND TRANSPORTING FISH

The catching and transporting of marine fish are the two prime difficulties you will encounter. Firstly, when catching fish other than those that inhabit rock pools, it is well to remember that a hooked fish is an injured fish. Only the lightly hooked fish should be placed in your tanks. Fish taken in trawls are often injured badly although they appear to be in good condition, but a friendly trawler skipper is the best contact any aquarist can wish for. If you can persuade him to take you with him when he is out trawling so much the better, for the best specimens as far as you are concerned are most frequently thrown back with the 'rubbish' from the cod-end.

Crab fishermen often get cuckoo wrasse, pouting and flatfish in their pots, besides a great variety of unexpected specimens, so if you know a crabber you are a long way towards getting some interesting specimens. You probably imagine that a trawlerman is an expert at keeping fish alive, but that is not so. It must be remembered that his primary job is to catch fish and deliver them to market. He never has to keep them alive. In consequence you will find it a good plan to mention tactfully certain facts concerning the keeping of fish in transit. The rules are simple and if adhered to your stock will survive long journeys.

Firstly never place more than one fish to 10 litres of water unless it is being constantly circulated—and you will be exceedingly lucky if those conditions prevail when you collect on a trawler. The water in the container should be changed as frequently as possible, simply by pouring a bucket of water into the can every half an hour, or more often if possible. Since few of you will ever possess oxygen cylinders or compressed-air cylinders we do not intend to say more than this. If you can get such cylinders charged at the local depot, then use them by all

Fig 25 Suitable fish for aquaria (*from top*) lesser spotted dogfish, bass,
ballan wrasse, fifteen-spined stickleback, great pipefish, rock goby

means, but it is a costly process, and one that few amateur aquarists will be inclined to do. Lastly, but perhaps the most important of all survival rules, *never handle your stock more than is absolutely essential.*

Lest the foregoing appears a too formidable list of difficulties, we hasten to add that the entire process is purely and simply common sense applied to the needs of your stock. The better you know their ways of life and the more you understand their requirements, the easier and more natural will be your treatment of them.

THE FISH

THE BLENNY (*Blennius pholis*). This precocious little fish is common in all rock pools where it will be found under rocks and rock ledges. It can be caught by using a net or secured with bare hands. Once in the aquarium it will settle down very quickly and by its very behaviour make itself a firm favourite. Blennies have a clownish appearance when viewed from the front, but their mode of moving more closely resembles that of a frog. They literally hop from place to place, except when in quest of a large ragworm, when they will hurtle across the tank before anything else can get near the food.

Blennies are easy to feed as they will take most kinds of sea life, but ragworm and mussel are firm favourites, and since the latter is easily come by, then it will probably be most used.

They will live with most animals, but will make short work of small shrimps, and will even attack tiny hermit crabs if hungry. Three ragworms or one mussel a week keeps a 3in specimen in good health, and the smaller fish can be given half-worms and pieces of mussel according to size. Blennies will also feed on small pieces of fresh fish such as whiting.

As a beginner's fish the blenny is ideal, for it is tolerant of a wide range of conditions and is readily adaptable. It will thrive in water far warmer than most species can stand, this being due to its habits of living in rock pools where sudden high temperatures are often experienced. It shows a marked preference for short spells out of water, and a suitable rock should be provided so that your fish can 'come up for an airing'. When visiting the tanks after dark we have often found the blennies resting on the top of rocks well out of the water; they do this regularly, and spend many of the dark hours in this way. If you happen to have a series of tanks in line, and the water level is high, you will find some of your blennies wandering from tank to tank. One specimen once moved through five tanks in less than a week, by wriggling up on to rocks and between airlines draped over the tank ends.

THE SPOTTED GOBY (*Gobius ruthensparri*). This is the small goby that is found swimming in small shoals amongst the fronds of *laminaria* and in many pools revealed by the ebbing tide. Essentially it is a species that swims in mid-water, and is seldom seen to keep to the bottom. When disturbed the entire shoal will race for shelter under weed fronds.

In aquaria they make ideal inhabitants, for they are extremely active and their mid-water swimming habits fill the tank with liveliness. When first introduced they invariably sulk under some rock for a couple of days. After that they are 'at home'.

It is a good plan to have a bivalve shell on the bottom of your tank, for the goby will adapt it for cover. Offered this sort of cover it will usually remain inside for a few hours at a time with its head protruding, or make sudden sallies around the tank.

Gobies are extremely hardy to temperature changes and can endure very low temperatures, but their oxygen requirements are great. When collecting or transporting this goby always aerate the water by stirring, for they will die in a jar if left for more than an hour in the hot weather.

Gobies show a preference for mussels as food and the pieces should be quite small and fed to them regularly.

THE LONG-SPINED SEA SCORPION (*Cottus bubalis*). This is an interesting species to keep, but due to its habit of swallowing everything that comes within reach, is best kept well away from other fish. It inhabits rock pools low on the shore and can be netted in some estuaries near to the sea.

Masters of camouflage, these creatures will change colour when first introduced to the tank and even their eyes have a disruptive pattern on them. When threatened, they extend their gills and this causes their heads to appear to swell. Hardy, hungry and fiercely competitive fish.

THE ROCK GOBY (*Gobius paganellus*). This is about the largest of the gobies and attains a length of nearly 3in. In captivity it is rather wild, tending to rush about and, unless the tank has a cover, jump out. One goby I kept was constantly jumping from one tank to another, and this sometimes happened as many as three times a day.

It is a species that delights in seeking cover, and unless this is provided it will seldom settle down in captivity to a natural life. Its appetite is enormous and one 4in fish can swallow half a large mussel at one gulp, so feed fairly liberally.

THE SAND GOBY (*Gobius minutus*). The smallest and most common of the gobies, it can be found in the shallowest of pools where it will be seen making sudden darts through the water and settling once more into obscurity.

Since it lives on the bottom and is so well camouflaged it is not a showy specimen for the tank. It is, however, very hardy, being accustomed to wide temperature ranges and sudden fluctuations of temperature in its natural rock-pool habitats. It will settle down well in the smallest tank, and for anyone who wishes to keep it alone with one or two of its own species nothing could be easier.

THE WRASSES (*Labridae*). Several species of wrasse are available for small aquaria, and generally speaking they make good tank inhabitants. They are primarily a rock-haunting fish and in their natural habitat seldom stray far from rock ledges where their food is found. Prawns, barnacles and small crabs are eaten avidly, and their stout teeth bear testimony to their diet.

Wrasse are one of the few species that sleep by night. To someone not used to their habits this can be disturbing, especially when the lights are suddenly turned on during the hours of darkness, for the fish will be found in the oddest of positions. Some rest on their tails with snout pointing upwards; some prefer to rest upside down; others will lie on their sides; others again lean at an angle of 45 degrees against some small rock and appear to have lost all sense of balance.

When swimming in the tank, wrasse are often most unfishlike. They will swim almost on their sides, or tilted so far over that you are likely to imagine some swim-bladder trouble is imminent. Doubtless such habits arise from their natural hunting along rock surfaces and the seeking of food in almost inaccessible places. In aquaria they are an extremely predatory species, and will attack small hermit crabs, many shellfish and worms and prawns, so it is as well to keep them away from such species. Small 2in wrasse kept in one tank cleared a whole colony of barnacles in a matter of a fortnight.

When first introduced this species often shows signs of tail damage. Characteristically this shows up as a tattered and very ragged tail fin, but in a very short time it will heal up and the tail grows to its former and more normal proportions.

Whilst wrasse feed readily on pieces of mussel there is little doubt that they thrive far better if their diet is supplemented with a certain amount of harder matter. In nature they consume many chitinous-bodied creatures and probably a certain quantity of roughage assists their normal digestion. When feeding on small shore crabs, the crab is held in the mouth for a matter of half a minute so that the teeth in the throat can get to work and detach the crab's back. This is then ejected and the rest of the animal swallowed whole.

In the sea, wrasse are seldom found in water around the rocks after the first frost, and it appears that they migrate out into deeper and warmer water during the winter. In an aquarium tank, however, they are quite hardy and can endure temperatures in the lower forties without undue distress. Below 40° F, however, they die, and the first signs of their discomfort is displayed when they lie on their sides at the bottom of the tank.

The commonest species you are likely to encounter is the ballan wrasse. It migrates inshore with the rising tide and is found under the weed along the rock-line. Generally green in colour when young their bodies glow with an iridescence that is quite attractive.

The most attractive of the wrasses is undoubtedly the cuckoo wrasse (*Labrus mixtus*) and the male in the breeding season is almost unbelievably brilliant. This species is highly prized for aquarium use, and can be obtained occasionally from crabbers, especially in the springtime.

The rock wrasse (*Ctenolabrus rupestris*) is coloured similarly to the common goldfish, but with a black spot at the base of the tail fin. It makes a rather attractive aquarium species due to its habit of swimming in small circles in mid-water—a place where movement is to be desired.

POLLACK (*Gadus pollachius*). Common around most coasts, the young are found in harbours during the summer months. These tiny fish, up to 5cm in length, will settle down well, and providing you can give them plenty of space make an attractive species when presented as a shoal. The small ones can be fed on almost any sort of fresh fish or animal matter, but mussel is preferred.

Large pollack when first introduced invariably 'sulk'. They steadfastly refuse food for up to two weeks or more, and it is as well to make no attempt to feed for the first week. Later they will take live prawns, ragworm, squid or mussel, or even pieces of white fish. Specimens up to 1in in length can be kept in a 4ft tank, and their constant slow swimming gives continuous movement.

If possible they should be fed on live food occasionally as there is no doubt that they thrive better when this is done.

THE BASS (*Morone labrax*). These attractive and beautiful fish are pugnacious by nature but will live with pollack and wrasse quite happily. At first they are not quick to settle down, and bass quickly show any wounds received as the result of careless handling. Such wounds show as red patches on the sides, reddening of the tail fin, or glossy white patches where scales have been lifted or lost.

Ragworms are an ideal food, but prawns and mussel are eaten as well. If none of these is available they will take white fish, but perseverance is necessary for many days before this is accepted.

In many river estuaries small bass will be found near the limit of the salt water well above the mouth. Here they range in size from 2in to 6in long, an ideal size for small tanks. Their diet can be supplemented with flies, although the larger ones will not be interested in such 'small fry'.

MULLET (*Mugilidae*). Small 2in specimens of young mullet can be found in rock pools in late summer and also in large shoals in estuaries and creeks. From observation it appears they feed on algae and soft animal food, but in the aquarium they enjoy crab meat or shredded uncooked fish or crushed mussel.

A shoal of small specimens make ideal aquarium fish as they stay swimming in mid-water and quickly become tame.

WHITING (*Gadus merlangus*). It is almost impossible to collect these in a net, and therefore they have to be caught on rod and line. As a direct result of their greedy feeding habits the hook is often well down the throat, and damage is often done. If undamaged specimens can be obtained they make excellent aquarium fish, for they are attractively coloured and feed readily on most kinds of food.

Since they tend to move inshore with the onset of cooler weather, it is to be expected that they will put up with lower temperatures better than the higher temperatures. Whiting have been kept for several months in water of below 40° F, although temperatures as low as this are not to be recommended.

POUTING (*Gadus luscus*). This handsome little fish can be caught on rod and line anywhere there are weed and rocks near to a sandy bottom. After the disturbance of being caught is overcome, they assume their normal banded coloration. With those black bands down their sides, and the white pelvic fins and trailing dorsal, they become excellent exhibits.

They are naturally greedy and need a little more food than most sea fish. They are not over-particular, and will take all the normal fish foods as well as earthworms. They are best kept by themselves, say four or five as a shoal, and when feeding it is as well to place the food in various parts of the tank, or else the largest fish will invariably gorge itself at the expense of the others. They tend to jump out of uncovered tanks—a habit difficult to explain in a species that lives on the bottom.

Pouting are often taken in crab pots, but these specimens are seldom any use to the aquarist, for when brought up from considerable depths their eyes are invariably affected and they have that typical 'pop-eye' appearance that cannot be cured.

YARREL'S BLENNY (*Chirolophis galerita*). This blenny grows to a considerable size, and in spite of this is a very timid species. A 10cm specimen will make sudden rushes at food as it descends through the water, but as long as any other fish is near it will retreat at once. One specimen regularly waited until all the rest of the inmates had fed before going for its own feed.

Normally it is a deep-water species but settles down in aquaria and gives little trouble, as it is extremely hardy.

THE BUTTERFLY BLENNY (*Blennius ocellaris*). This is a small blenny with an attractive habit of nesting in large shells. Specimens at a marine laboratory often nest in old Bovril bottles! In the breeding season they should be provided with some sort of natural retreat in which to deposit their eggs. They are hardy in aquaria providing the temperature does not go below 40°.

BUTTERFISH OR GUNNEL (*Centronotus gunnellus*). An attractive reddish-brown eel-shaped fish with a line of black spots along its back, found frequently under rocks in shallow pools where it often lives in empty shells. In the aquarium it always seeks some sort of cover. If you can provide an empty whelk shell it will probably settle in it. Food is tiny pieces of fish.

THE WEEVERS—THE LESSER WEEVER (*Trachinus vipera*). As its Latin name suggests, this fish is a rather unpleasant species to handle. It has a black dorsal fin armed with strong spines which can penetrate the skin and release poison into your hand. The resulting wound is both painful and dangerous, so beware when handling. Its natural habitat is in the sand along the shore and here it will bury and wait for food. When introduced to a tank it at once tries to burrow down with a rapid digging movement of the pectoral fins.

It is not a hardy species in aquaria, and due to its unpleasant habits not the best of fish for the beginner, or in any home where children have access to the tank.

FLATFISH. Various members of this family can be kept with varying degrees of success in small aquaria up to 4ft in length.

The hardiest of these is the topknot (*Zeugopterus punctatus*), and hand-sized specimens of this little flatfish will live for a long time if fed on live prawns. When kept in a tank with other more active fish such as pollack and bass, it often has to go short of food. To prevent this happening it is best to feed it by hand, and this can be done by holding the prawn by its antennae and keeping it thus out of the way of the other fish. A topknot will soon learn to take food from the hand.

Flounders (*Pleuronectes flesus*) and plaice (*Pleuronectes platessa*) are two more species that can be kept successfully, especially if young specimens can be found, and whilst they show a preference for worm, they will take small prawns and other food if these are not available.

Generally speaking the flatfish family is not an active one, and tends to be rather unpredictable in its longevity, but such failings are compensated for in its extremely interesting swimming movements and eye movements.

SKATE or RAY (*Raiidae*) and DOGFISH (*Scyliorhinus canicula*). These are best left alone in small aquaria, although small ones will sometimes settle down. They are extremely difficult to get on the feed. Young dogfish of various species are common in all trawl hauls, but again quite tricky in small tanks. In spite of their voracious habits in the sea they steadfastly refuse food when kept in captivity. A 15in specimen can be kept in a 4ft tank if it is fed on pieces of fish, and can be trained to take it from the hand. There is no doubt that this species would rather take its food in mid-water than from the bottom, and you should feed it by holding a piece of food in the fingers and trailing it through the water; you will find the dogfish following up the scent trail, and eventually it will approach and turn on its side to take the food.

CONGER (*Conger vulgaris*). Sooner or later every marine aquarist has to try a conger eel, and the smaller the better for small tanks. Provide some sort of pipe so that it can retreat within and make its home there, for this eel delights in having some sort of cover.

The 6-10in conger will often be found under rocks at low tide, and these little fellows have an unfortunate habit of burying themselves in the sand and disappearing from sight for long spells at a time. After dark they will be found with their heads protruding apparently waiting for food. All congers are experts at getting out of tanks, so a firm cover is essential and it must be tight-fitting. A variety of food can be used, but they must all be fresh.

PIPEFISH (*Syngnathidae*). Pipefish can be found low on the shore in the *laminaria* pools, and in summer they come right inshore and will be found much higher up. They feed on plankton and small forms of life. In aquaria they *must* be offered live foods as they will only take a *moving* creature; the ideal food is mysis, whose method of collection is discussed later.

Pipefish collected before June will often spawn in the tank. The eggs are carried by the male in a pouch on the stomach and retained until the young hatch. The young are then released to swim into the sea. Feeding these tiny pin-sized fish is a real problem and for most aquarists it will be a wise policy to release them into the sea.

FIFTEEN-SPINED STICKLEBACK (*Spinachia vulgaris*). This is another plankton-feeder with much the same problem for the aquarist as the pipefish. It is a very attractive species in its habits, but feeding difficulties are insurmountable unless you are prepared to collect live food such as mysids or small—very small—prawns.

OTHER SPECIES. The variety of fish has only just been touched upon. There are many not mentioned that may be encountered and attempted, but the foregoing list contains those that are known to be suited to aquarium conditions. The problems of the small-scale aquarist are much greater than those of the large public aquaria, and many species that can be kept successfully in large tanks will not thrive in small tanks.

As has been stressed throughout this book, there is ample room for experiment, and aquarists taking up marine aquaria must realise that they are attempting one of the most worthwhile forms of fish-keeping. Little has been written on the actual mechanics of the job, but there is no doubt at all that an ounce of practical experience is worth a ton of theory. And finally, what goes for a man living in one region may well not apply to another region.

Whilst fish, as such, are the most difficult form of marine life to keep, they will thrive if due care and attention is given to every detail of their requirements. Not least of these should be an endeavour to create a habitat as near to their natural one as possible. Shade for shade lovers; shelter for timid ones; sand for sandy-shore species and stones for rocky-shore specimens.

11

FOODS AND FEEDING

In various parts of this book will be found notes on the feeding of certain species, but there still remains much to be said on this matter. And, the aquarist living some distance from the sea has problems that will seldom arise with someone living close to the shore.

One great misconception is very widely held: countless people believe that the creatures that can be kept in a marine aquarium tank need food every day.

Marine creatures develop more troubles through overfeeding than through underfeeding.

The vast majority of your specimens will thrive and remain healthy if fed twice a week in winter and three times a week in summer. With the wide range of animals available to the marine aquarist, it is impossible to lay down hard-and-fast rules for quantities to be given at a single meal, but there is one sure way of judging the amount. It is simply to feed a number of small pieces until such time as the animal shows little inclination to eat. It has then had enough, and any extra food placed in that tank will merely be overfeeding.

From experience one soon learns that most sea animals can live quite happily without food for as long as a week or more, and not long ago the author decided to try a few experiments in the aquarium feeding of animals of various kinds. A number of lessons were learned and these are enumerated below.

1. Crustaceans will thrive if fed only once a week. The

water in their tank will remain clearer and secondary troubles from overfeeding will then be cut to a minimum.

2. Fish fed only once a week during the summer tend to keep far more active than those fed three times a week.

3. Various starfish fed once a fortnight thrived and lived far longer than those that were fed more frequently.

4 In winter if the tank temperature drops considerably it is advisable to feed once every ten days.

5. Fish requiring live food must be fed more frequently; if a small amount should be offered, say, once every other day.

FEEDING FRESHLY INTRODUCED SPECIMENS

Whenever new fish are placed in the tank leave them without any food for at least three days, and sometimes a week is better. In winter most species are slow to start feeding, and in summer some species will not take food for as long as three weeks. Such behaviour has little effect on their general health, although pollack have been observed to go quite thin during the first settling-down period. Crustaceans will usually feed quite quickly after introduction, as they appear to be much more adaptable to a change of habitat. The octopus sometimes feeds during the first night of arrival.

Generally speaking then, there is no need to worry over any marine animal that refuses food during the initial stages of settling-down. After that it is primarily a question of getting to know the requirements of your particular specimens and feeding in accordance with their demands.

FOODSTUFFS

NATURAL FOODS. No food can equal the natural feed of the species. For many aquarists living inland this is a doctrine of perfection that cannot be followed, and a modification is essential.

Firstly, there are the marine foods to be considered. Mussels rank high as a food for practically every species of fish and all manner of sea creatures. The entire shellfish can be fed to craw-fish; a whole mussel, providing it has been opened, will be consumed by a large blenny; crushed mussel is a perfect food for many of the so-called plankton-feeders such as plumose anemones. Mussels (*Mytilus edulis*) are easy to collect from most rocky areas, pier piles and harbour walls. They can be stored in a glass jar without water for as long as ten days providing they are kept cool.

Another excellent food is prawns (*Leander* spp) (and for the present purpose shrimps are included). Many small fish will take live shrimps or tiny prawns, and for those species, such as wrasse, that are used to a hard diet, they provide some of the roughage necessary for normal digestion. Large prawns can be cut up into smaller pieces and left unskinned for many marine creatures, although baby mullet prefer peeled prawns.

Whilst worms are a natural food of many species there are certain disadvantages in using them in aquaria. They tend to foul the water, and species such as lugworm are really trouble-some if used as food. Ragworm, in areas where they are easily obtained, make a useful supplement to any feeding plan and will be taken by most sea fish.

Other live foods that can be tried include sand-hoppers (*Amphipoda*), various shellfish and crabs. Sand-hoppers are best collected at night with the aid of a powerful paraffin pressure lamp. The lamp should be placed on a part of the beach known to be inhabited by this species, and two holes dug at the side of the lamp and close to its base. Into these holes are sunk two jam jars so that their tops are level with the top of the sand. Within five minutes of lighting the lamp, providing you have selected a good place, the sand around the lamp's illuminated area will swarm with the jumping bodies of sand-hoppers—and large numbers of these will fall into the jars. A useful tip, if you prefer to leave the lamp for half an hour, is to place small paper funnels in the top of the jars, so that once the sand-hoppers slide down into the jars, they cannot jump out again.

Small shore crabs make good food for some fish, and have the great advantage of being very easy to collect.

Mysids are an excellent food. They resemble very small thin prawns and are found in the tidal parts of rivers. The best time to collect them is at high water, when, due to the absence of a strong current, the mysids gather against walls, slipways, steps and the like, and can be netted with any *small*-mesh net. They can be kept alive if *small numbers* are placed in plastic containers with some water from the collecting site and kept aerated all the time.

FOODS AVAILABLE TO THE INLAND AQUARIST. When it is not possible to collect food from the seashore, one of the best foods is white fish, such as gurnard or whiting. Cut into small pieces and wash before placing in the tank, as this removes most of the loose scraps that always result from cutting fish. Never use any oily fish as this will quickly cause pollution troubles. The worst offenders are mackerel and herring.

Pieces of cooked crab meat will be appreciated as a change of diet, and many species of crustacean will take ordinary common earthworms. Woodlice are eaten by a few species of fish, whilst that popular fresh-water food, daphnia, is taken eagerly.

Shredded raw meat can be used to feed anemones and some crabs will go for it, although there is always the odd one that shows little inclination to try such unusual food.

Uncooked frozen fish, providing the batter or breadcrumbs are first removed, will also be taken and apparently enjoyed.

SIMPLE RULES FOR FEEDING

1. Never feed more than once every three days.
2. Underfeed rather than overfeed.
3. Remove all uneaten food scraps within two hours of feeding.

Remember that any sea animal with a healthy appetite is a far better proposition than polluted water and gastric disorders. Feeding, like seeding, must not be done too thickly—or the stock will decline.

Few disorders will occur of the stock if cared for and kept

under good conditions, but a really sick or diseased fish is far better if returned to the sea. Everything in the sea is prey to some parasite or predator and the variety of these is almost unlimited. Yet in spite of, or perhaps because of, such a difficult existence only the strong survive.

12

THE PATH TO DISCOVERY

Most of us who have learned a little about one or two marine creatures, and who have tried to discover some secret hidden beneath the restless sea, have been bitten by the unrelenting curiosity to learn more. The study of the sea, and marine biology, is one of the youngest sciences, yet its advance has been rapid and the story of life beneath the water is emerging. A few contributions to this story have been made by amateur naturalists.

Much of this investigation has been carried out in aquaria, and providing the aquarium conditions are made as near as possible to natural conditions, the behaviour of the animal under observation will not be greatly different from its normal mode of life.

In the first place, perhaps, few aquarists will want to publish scientific papers, but for the large number who do want to develop their interest in the study of sea life there is endless scope. But how to begin? There is a wide variety of methods, but first and foremost the importance of *recording every observation*, either by writing notes or sketching, must be emphasised. It is surprising how even the most interesting observation becomes dulled by time if it is not recorded. Once in the notebook, however, it can be frequently amplified by future observations and some inexplicable incident becomes perfectly clear.

One of the greatest traps for the naturalist is to start on a certain path of investigation with a preconceived theory about what is going to happen. Never do this, for when your observations show theory to be wrong it is all too easy to ignore the truth. Try to get as much pleasure out of proving a theory wrong as from getting a set of concurrent observations in perfect agreement.

But perhaps you will still be wondering where to begin recording your observations? At risk of stating the obvious, let it be said that the starting point must always be . . . WHY? Why does that hermit crab miss a piece of food dropped behind its shell when it can detect another piece 12in away? If we take that as an example, we can see there is an immediate field for experiment. For instance, is it because the hermit *saw* one piece and not the other? Is it because some *other sense* is involved? If so, what other sense? Can scent be a cause? You can go on asking questions *ad infinitum*, and finding the correct answers to them will require hours of observation, and add great interest to your hobby.

There are a host of incidental records that can be kept, and as a beginning you might be able to keep temperature records of the shore pools to find if there is any apparent correlation between temperature and the offshore movement of species.

The biggest hindrance to the would-be observer seems to be a fear that 'all this is a waste of time because somebody must have done it all before'. But such is not the case, because if by 'somebody' you wish to imply those who work professionally in marine biological laboratories, you would soon discover that their time is so filled that there is just not enough time to do everything. I have been fortunate enough to spend many hours with prominent biologists, and the more I speak with them, the more I learn how much is still to be unravelled. For the seas are vast and the science of the seas is young and the number working on the problems is small. Here, then, is the opportunity for the marine aquarist to engage in original work of the most interesting and valuable kind—reporting actual observations.

Strict honesty is of course essential, intellectual honesty above all. It is all too easy to develop a theory from some chance observation, and to nurture it into a supposed fact, without constant repetitive observations to support it. Have a theory by all means, but be prepared and willing to discard it at the first instance of deviation. When this deviation occurs, follow it up just as relentlessly, until your observations lead you to some conclusive proof. Perhaps few things *are* conclusive in the seas, for life there cannot be observed easily in its natural surroundings, and most of our work will be governed by the varying factor of aquarium conditions. For those who wish to progress beyond the aquarium into the open 'field' of rock pools and seas there lies a wonderful prospect of discovery. Where else on earth can so varying a habitat be found as that of a single group of inshore rocks? From splash zone to low-tide limits is a constantly changing habitat and the manner in which so many of the animals have adapted themselves to these changes still remain unknown.

The chief trouble is that the shore offers too much to observe, and too often we wander away from our particular subject. Whilst this is perfectly good for the keen naturalist who wishes to become acquainted with shore life, it is of little use to the more serious study of a species. There will be many occasions when while following up one species we encounter the effects of a second or third species, for all shore life is integrated, and each species modifies the behaviour of another in some way. In the limited space available it is not possible to enlarge on this, but in the book list will be found some excellent books of reference which can be used by the shore collector.

As long as books are used for reference they can be of inestimable value, but in the field of natural history there is a distressing tendency to 'take for granted that what is written is correct'. Rely primarily on your own recorded observations, and then if you so wish you can check with a book to see whether 'so and so' is known. If the written word of the book differs from your own records, it is worth while following up, for then you may make your own small, but original, contribution to knowledge of shore life.

The first great seashore observer was Philip Henry Gosse. He lived a hundred years ago, but his writings are classics of observational work. Gosse never lost the freshness of excitement that came from some new discovery, and his appetite for knowledge was insatiable. If you desire, as did Gosse's friend Charles Kingsley in *Glaucus*, to 'walk on and in under the waves' you will have found a new and absorbing interest in your aquarium.

13

BREEDING

The time may well arrive when an opportunity presents itself for the breeding of some species from the egg. In the early spring, creatures such as sea slugs readily deposit eggs on the walls and rocks, but little can be done to ensure their successful growth.

For the aquarist wishing to try rearing from the egg, it is a good idea to start with something relatively easy, such as, for instance, the egg of a dogfish (*Scyliorhinus* spp). These can be obtained from various biological laboratories, or trawlermen can be persuaded to bring specimens in. The dogfish is particularly interesting because the egg case is semi-transparent and the embryo can be observed through its growth. The eggs take anything up to nine months to develop, so a long period of time is available for observation. Throughout this period the embryo will feed exclusively on the large yolk-sac within the egg case, and the only attention that is required is occasionally to wash off the dirt that collects so that the embryo can be seen. *At such times keep the egg case under water and handle with due care.*

REARING OF DOGFISH FROM THE EGG
(*Scyliorhinus canicula*)

Trawlermen frequently make large catches of dogfish and every so often one of the specimens will have the tell-tale threads of the capsule trailing from its body. This is a sign the egg is ripe, and for some hours after the dogfish is dead, this egg capsule remains alive. By simply slitting the outside skin of the dead fish, the egg capsule will be found within the oviduct. It can be released and hung by the threads in an aquarium. For about six to eight weeks it remains clear, and development of the embryo can be observed, but slowly the capsule darkens. At this stage the embryo can be transferred to a plastic capsule, made as follows:

Take any thin clear plastic, such as perspex; the material used to provide improvised glazing for greenhouses is ideal (not polythene). Cut this with scissors to a shape similar to that of the real capsule, but a little longer. The front piece should be cut a little larger than the rear face.

Next you need glue, and the best for this work is Bostik 1, but any clear adhesive that 'welds' or bonds perspex will do. Place two of the edges together and hold with a clothes peg whilst placing a thin strip of adhesive along the edges. Leave to dry thoroughly. When dry, push the larger surface until the edges match up on the unglued side and again hold with pegs. Glue this second edge. Leave to dry.

Cut a small piece to fit the open space at the bottom, glue it in place. The artificial capsule is now complete.

TRANSFER OF LIVING EMBRYO. This must not be attempted until at least six weeks after the egg was removed from the female dogfish. Any attempt to do this earlier will result in the rupture of the yolk.

Part-fill a basin with sea water. Cut off one end of the capsule just below the two projections from which spring the threads. Now with your other hand pick up the plastic capsule. Place the open ends of the capsules together: if you made the plastic one a little larger, then the living capsule can be placed *inside* the open end of the plastic one. Apply gentle pressure at the far end of the living capsule and with a little luck the embryo and yolk will pass smoothly into the plastic capsule.

It takes a certain knack to be successful, but the skill lies in being careful, patient and gentle. Having transferred many embryos in this way I can vouch for the ease of the operation.

Providing the transferred embryo is kept in diffused light and is hung by a cotton thread in the aquarium, the entire development of the dogfish can be observed. Eventually the fully developed little fish will swim free—or can be released—and can be reared in the tank until too large, when it can finally be returned to the sea.

Whelk (*Buccinum undatum*) eggs can easily be obtained from fishermen, and in many cases will hatch successfully without attention. The young, as they emerge, are well worth study under the magnifying glass.

Some years ago we had the good fortune to rear some young bass (*Morone labrax*) from the egg, and providing you are able to secure the eggs from a large public aquarium or marine laboratory it is a memorable experience to attempt such a project. First we assume that you can obtain the eggs. Ours came from a public aquarium where a shoal of bass had spawned.

Prepare your aquarium by removing all sand from the floor, as this will tend to trap some of the pelagic eggs and cause them to die. Really strong circulation by good aeration is the next requirement, so that every egg is kept constantly on the move.

In the case of the pelagic eggs of the bass, the infertile or dead ones quickly sink to the bottom, whilst the living ones remain circulating in the upper water. Remove all dead eggs as soon as possible. They can usually be distinguished by having a tiny speck of dull white within the nucleus, or sometimes the entire egg goes opaque. Developing eggs remain perfectly transparent, and the young embryo can be seen quite plainly under the microscope. Development is rapid in many fish eggs, and in the case of bass the young hatch in five days.

At first the post-larval fish is equipped with a comparatively large yolk-sac which will provide its food for the ensuing ten days or so. After this it has to feed on plankton, and without doubt this is a great difficulty for the aquarist to overcome. Plankton can be collected as described in Chapter 6, but the catch must be rigorously sorted to exclude all the larger and possibly predatory forms that may well attack and eat your more valuable post-larval fish.

As soon as the young fish commence to swim actively, and this is normally within a week of hatching, then is the time to slow down the air circulation. Violent movement is no longer necessary, although plentiful aeration must be continued. The exact and happy medium is not easily attained. To sum up this aeration business: For *eggs*, the entire volume of water in the tank must be kept on the move, so that every single egg is being kept moving around the tank throughout the twenty-four hours. The *young* require less movement, so the air pressure must be lowered until only the faintest, but nevertheless continuous, water circulation can be observed.

One of the greatest enemies of the aquarist trying to rear sea-fish eggs is high temperature or variations up or down. Temperatures of up to 60° F are reasonably safe providing such temperatures can be kept steady, and this is not always easy when the aquarium has to be kept in a living-room where doors and windows create draughts.

Firstly, then, the aquarium must be kept well away from these draughts, and secondly it must be so placed as to ensure that no direct sunlight shines on it. As is often the case in early spring, the days are warm, but at night the temperature falls. In your living-room when any form of heating is turned off at night, the temperature will drop sufficiently to kill eggs or post-larval fish. It has been found that a drop of 2° or 3°, if it takes place within an hour, is sufficient to cause considerable loss. Therefore if you can keep direct draughts or sunlight away, you are well set for successful rearing.

Another type of rearing that can be attempted is with hermit crabs. Usually by the middle of February these crabs will have well-developed egg masses attached to their bodies within the shell. The crabs can be seen resting on the tank bottom and extending their bodies from the shell, so as to expose the egg masses to the freely circulating surrounding water. They will move their bodies in and out and sideways, keeping the eggs on the move. Then one day you will perhaps be fortunate enough to see the tiny zoea or young larvae of the crab swim free into the open water, for in this instance the eggs are not released. The zoea develop within the egg and when ready emerge to spend their short lives drifting with the other plankton.

It is during early spring that many of the seashore animals lay their eggs, and a wide and varying number of species will be found among the rock pools at this time. Egg clusters will be found on rock ledges, attached to seaweed, on the under-surface of rocks and empty shells and a host of less obvious places (Fig 26). These can be collected, but due care must be exercised when removing them or they will be damaged. When you transfer them to the aquarium, always endeavour to place them in a position as near as possible to the place where they were found.

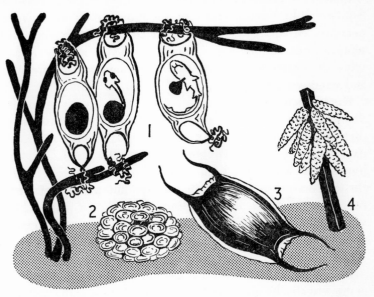

Fig 26   1 dogfish eggs showing development of embryo; 2 whelk eggs; 3 skate eggs; 4 squid eggs

In all the literature written about the seashore and its life, one finds very little information on the actual breeding of marine creatures under aquarium conditions. This field has been fairly well explored, but all too often the biologists concerned are more interested in the stages of the creatures being reared than in the actual mechanics of the operation. For the aquarist with determination, here lies a wide field for experiment, and one where a great deal of original work can be carried out. Without doubt the primary difficulty is to provide accommodation large enough for adult fish, and then to get fertilisation of the egg. Whilst many fish may well be difficult for the small-scale aquarist, there is plenty of scope with the common species of the rock pools.

REARING SMALL FISH

On occasions the aquarist and collector will probably chance upon a shoal of small fish in some rock pool. During the summer months of June to September, for instance, there are always plenty of mullet in such places, especially around the fringes of rocks.

With a species like mullet (*Mugilidae*), 80 per cent of your rearing troubles are solved if you have a tank with a luxuriant growth of weed in it. They will browse quite happily and only need their vegetarian diet supplemented with mashed fish or fish liver. As many as thirty 1½in mullet can be kept in a 12in tank and they will thrive if fed about three times a week.

Small pollack (*Gadidae*) are good fish to rear as well, but as their diet is exclusively carnivorous you must supply sufficient in the form of grated liver or grated fish. A 2in pollack needs feeding every other day with regularity and the amount given should equal the size of two match-heads. Increase the quantity as it grows according to the avidity with which the food is taken.

Small whiting and other such species can all be reared in aquaria, but for the beginner nothing could be easier than mullet providing there is ample algae on the tank walls.

Once again one fact must be stressed. Few aquarists have written up the results of how certain species were reared—but there is no doubt that a certain amount of experience is essential. Experience with ordinary small marine aquaria should be the starting point, and this, plus patience, will lead to good results.

14

THE MARINE MUSEUM, AND NOTES ON METHODS OF PREPARING AND PRESERVING SPECIMENS

*Conservation of living plants and animals
and not collection must be the keynote*

If we collect ruthlessly, the narrow band of rich beauty we call the seashore will soon become a place with few species; it is all too easy to destroy life and so very difficult to *conserve* it.

It is an outdated hobby to collect living specimens for preservation, so for this purpose use only dead material found on the shore and tide-line. Aquarists must strive to increase the numbers of each species on the seashore and zealously guard their habitat from human intrusion.

Those who have walked along the shores after a storm has sent its flotsam and jetsam in great piles along the drift-line, will appreciate what a rich collecting ground this can be. Some of the commonest items will be discarded egg cases of skate and dogfish, the 'bone' of the cuttlefish, worm-ridden timbers, and tubeworm-covered shells and corks.

Besides these more common objects you will often find a rare shell with its occupant still alive. In all probability it will not be possible to keep the specimen alive for long, but if you are keen, and follow the ideas suggested in this chapter, you will be able to start a collection that will be an ever-growing source of interest both to yourself and to those who call to see your aquarium.

Briefly the idea is to start a museum. We know all too well that the word museum has unfortunately developed a layer of dust upon itself and implies everything that is dead. But the finest museums present their collections in a lively way that can rival any living show—and with a little care and practice you can do the same.

But to give an example. You find a shell of *natica* with the occupant alive inside. Instead of boiling out the specimen and mounting the shell on a piece of cardboard or placing it in a case, you set out to make a worthwhile exhibit. Firstly, since the creature is alive put it in one of your tanks. Watch it, and if you are any good with a pencil make a few rapid sketches, no matter how rough they may be. In this way you can keep a record of the living animal so that later you can make a model. It is really much better to construct a small set-up showing the creature in its natural habitat and caught in the attitude of actually doing something, than to have an empty shell with the name recorded neatly underneath.

The animals themselves can be constructed from barbola paste or papier mâché. For those not acquainted with these two media, it may be advisable to give some notes. Papier mâché can be made from newspaper, by tearing it into tiny pieces smaller than a postage stamp. The smaller you tear the pieces, the smoother will be your finished work. Having torn up sufficient paper to make the required model, place the pieces in a saucepan of boiling water and boil for half an hour, leave in the water for twenty-four hours and then boil again for a further hour. Remove the saucepan from the heat and with a stirring rod reduce the paper to a pulp. When this has cooled down, pour into a piece of cotton cloth and squeeze all moisture from it.

The next process is to place this semi-dry pulp in a basin and add a small amount of thick paper-hanger's paste, stirring it well in with a wooden spoon, until the entire pulp is of the consistency of porridge. Next add powdered whiting until the pulp turns to the stiffness of putty, and you are ready to commence modelling.

Barbola paste is bought in tins ready for use, and although a little more costly is the ideal medium for modelling small objects; since it is less absorbent, when dry, than papier mâché it is much easier to paint.

Now let us assume we have collected an empty *natica* shell. Make quite sure the shell is perfectly clean and that all pieces have been removed from within. You will now need a small quantity of plaster of paris and a piece of wire about 2in long. Place your shell upside down in a matchbox so as to prevent it tipping sideways. Take the piece of wire and twist one end into irregular shape so that it fits inside the opening of the shell. Place the wire in this opening with the straight end pointing outwards.

You are now ready to pour the plaster of paris in, and incidentally, make quite sure you do not mix this until all the preceding operations have been carried out. Pour the plaster in until it is level with the lips of the shell opening, and leave to dry. Within twenty-four hours it will be ready for the next process.

What you have really done so far is to make a secure fixture for the model of the shellfish, so that it can be secured in place when it is finished.

With regard to the actual modelling of the specimen no amount of written advice can equal a little practical work—so have a try at it and you will be surprised how easy it is to get a good likeness of the creature you are modelling. Whether it be papier mâché or barbola, each is moulded with the fingers and with the aid of a sharply pointed piece of bamboo. To save materials you can always build up your model over a framework of cork or wood.

When the animal is finished to your liking, place it in a warm dry atmosphere to dry off. Finally it is secured to the shell by pushing it over the wire end and gluing into place with liberal quantities of aero glue. Painted with ordinary watercolour and finished with a coat of brushing cellulose, the effect is complete.

In spite of that explanation, you still have only a model of the *natica* you watched in your aquarium! It now remains to set it up to show a more interesting side of its life.

For the base plate use a piece of hardboard or three-ply, cut to a predetermined size. Mount your model on this with the aid of glue, and since you are showing *natica*, heap some pebbles all around it to give the effect of its bulldozing progress through the sand in search of a victim. Below this model you can then mount a further model to show how *natica* attacks its victim, and below this again mount a few shells with the tell-tale holes in them where the proboscis of *natica* sucked out their living bodies. A few explanatory labels will complete a good exhibit. The best way to discover the secrets of *natica*'s life is, of course, to watch it in your aquarium, but since this is not always possible, the facts can be read up. All that is then required is a little imagination and plenty of patience.

The foregoing lengthy explanation has been made because no matter what type of museum set-piece you choose to make, the same basic system can be adopted.

Small crustaceans can be preserved in another way. Walking the tide-line you will encounter a number of dead specimens, especially after periods of rough seas. Take the dead animal and set it out on a piece of cork or balsa wood in such a position that it looks reasonably natural. This can be achieved by judicious placing of pins to hold limbs and antennae in position—in much the same way as the old collectors of moths and butterflies would set out their specimens. When you are satisfied that the animal is ready, place it in a warm oven and leave for about eight hours. This is usually long enough to dry out such creatures as large hermit crabs, prawns and small crabs.

When first removed from the oven the specimen will be exceedingly brittle and it is advisable to apply a thick coating of aero glue to all joints to give added strength. A final double coating of brushing cellulose will further add durability. Specimens such as these can be mounted in dioramas and make ideal exhibits for use in schools or for your own personal collection.

For 'atmosphere' and effects required to make up a habitat in diorama, use the real thing whenever possible. If you want seaweed, then use seaweed. Dry it off and restore its colour with powder paint. Artificial rockwork can be made from papier mâché if lightness is a consideration, but never carry the modelling habit too far. Nothing looks worse than an attempt at reality that thrusts its artificiality at the viewer.

Models of the soft-bodied creatures can be made from barbola or papier mâché, as previously indicated.

Making a collection of seashells is well worthwhile, but care is needed in the preparation and presentation of your shells. All kinds of 'dead' shells will be found along the tide-line, and these should be placed for cleaning in a bucket of water to which a cupful of household bleach has been added. Leave for twenty-four hours and then wash in several changes of tap water until all traces of bleach have been removed. Place the shells on newspaper to dry.

Shells can be kept in various ways, either loosely in polythene bags, cardboard boxes or plastic containers, or mounted on thick card, hardboard or wood. Use a good strong adhesive (such as Bostik 1 or Araldite). When all the specimens are mounted their appearance will be considerably improved if they are varnished with a cellulose or polyurethane clear varnish. This restores their true colours and enhances the general appearance of your collection.

Specimens of worm-ridden timber and other flotsam can be dried out slowly and similarly treated with cellulose. It is as well to remember that all your specimens once came from the sea, and the shiny appearance given by a coat of this varnish brings back the sea-lustre to your collection and makes it much more lifelike.

Take a look through a microscope at the contents of a filter paper after filtering a few drops of sea water, or better still examine your plankton haul. In the eye-piece of your microscope you will find sufficient of interest to keep you busy for many a winter's night. Diatoms with intricate patterns, fantastic zoea, and other surrealist creatures that can be made into large models of great interest will be found.

PRESERVATION OF SPECIMENS

Under no circumstances should living creatures be collected for preservation purposes—it is an archaic and totally unacceptable method of making a collection.

Notes on the preservation of marine specimens are scattered through all manner of volumes, and many of these prescriptions use dangerous drugs and are expensive in any quantity. After a number of years experimenting with a wide variety of marine creatures, we are convinced that one of the simplest and cheapest methods is to use formalin. This can be purchased from any chemist. Buy it in concentrated form, and all you have to do is to add it to the water later. Fish, worms, crabs and other picturesque animals like the sea-mouse can be preserved in this solution. Fish will retain their colour, and providing a fish such as a mackerel is fresh when introduced to the medium the bright colours will last for months.

The system is as follows. Take a clean glass container with an airtight lid, such as a preserving jar, or one of the specimen jars obtainable from any biological supply house. Ordinary oven-ware cooking dishes are ideal, providing a glass cover can be secured in place by a layer of glue or some other adhesive, like a rubber compound. Having well washed your specimen in tap water, place it in position in the container. Pour on a measured quantity of fresh water and to this add one-fortieth part of formalin. Place the lid in position and leave for a week or two. Then remove the lid, rewash the specimen, throw away the first solution and re-immerse in a fresh solution made in exactly the same proportions. The specimen can then be left indefinitely, providing the container is airtight.

If the specimen is to be seen through the top cover, as will be the case with those preserved in ovenware dishes, there will be a certain amount of trouble from condensation. This can be overcome by filling the container right to the very top, or by merely reversing the container before examining the contents. No condensation difficulties will be experienced when the object is to be viewed through the sides, for obvious reasons.

Seaweeds can be preserved in this medium, but they tend to lose their colour after a time, although the specimens will remain otherwise perfect. The red weeds particularly soon lose their colour, and this will diffuse into the preservative, making the entire specimen rather obscure. If the preservative is changed regularly in the initial stages, clarity will soon be achieved.

To repeat the formula:

Concentrated formalin	$2\frac{1}{2}$ per cent
Clean tap water	$97\frac{1}{2}$ per cent

Certain marine animals, such as the squid and cuttlefish, will preserve well in a saturated salt solution: simply take a quantity of tap water and add salt to it until no more will dissolve. It is amazing how much salt will dissolve in water, so make sure you keep going until you reach saturation point. Let the solution settle, so that excess salt settles on the bottom of your container, and then pour the clear solution into the preserving bottle. Fish preserved in this way tend to lose colour much more quickly than those in formalin, although worms preserve well.

Lastly a word of warning to those who seek a more complex formula for specialised use. Many of these formulae are intended for use where the specimen has to keep indefinitely without regard to its colour. If such is your aim then use these formulae by all means. But if you wish to preserve a specimen for a couple of years and no more, then you will find the simple one quoted here is the best of all.

15

A LARGE PUBLIC AQUARIUM: THE PLYMOUTH AQUARIUM

This is the aquarium of the Marine Biological Association UK, and is internationally accepted as a first class public aquarium. Many of the constructional features will be of interest and practical use to hobbyists anywhere in the world.

In planning the aquarium the main objectives have been:

1. provision of the best possible conditions for the animals;
2. provision for the viewer of as natural-looking scene as possible in each tank, well-illuminated and with no 'works' showing;
3. ease of maintenance and day-to-day servicing.

The first of these objectives has always taken precedence over the other two and the second almost always over the third. Only in this way can a healthy and attractive aquarium be attained. In addition, the public hall and its approaches have been made as well-proportioned and pleasing as possible.

BASIC CONSTRUCTION OF THE TANKS

The tanks are constructed of reinforced concrete of aluminous cement mixed with local sands and aggregates. Internal surfaces of the back walls and parts of the side walls were subsequently rendered with a waterproof cement and sand mix to seal off hair-cracks.

The larger tanks on the north and south sides are 6ft wide (front to back) and 4ft deep, with a water depth of 3ft 6in. Their walls are 6–7in thick, their bottoms 8–9in thick. Creosoted soft-boards used when casting the back walls of the tanks, to prevent the concrete adhering to the walls of the building, remain in position. The big tank at the east end is internally 29ft long and varies in width from about 8ft 4in at the centre to about 9ft 3in near each end. The bottom of this tank is about 10in thick, and at the north end it drops down to a lower level over an area irregular in shape, thereby increasing the water depth at this place by about 1ft 3in.

The small tanks with a water depth of rather less than 2ft 6in occupy the corners between the ends of the big tank and the north- and south-side series. On the north side at the west end a shallow triangular tank overlaps a floor tank which is divisible into two with a removable partition or, as at present, by built-in rockwork. The floor tank is viewed only through the water surface and is designed for the display of flatfishes on contrasted bottom shingles. Except for this floor tank the water surface in all the tanks is at a uniform height.

Except for the shallower tanks all the window openings are of uniform size, 5ft 7½in long by 3ft high. One advantage of this uniformity is that a single spare pane of glass fits all tanks except the shallow ones. The glass panes, 1in thick, overlap the window opening 1½in all round. These openings are formed of slate inserts keyed to the concrete. The slates are grooved to give facings exactly 1½in wide. This is necessary to achieve uniformity of pressure on the sealing compound and to aid in positioning the glass. The glass is pressed by water pressure against sealing compound Glasticon (Glasticord 304), laid in strip form on the facings. A single teak turnbuckle fixed to the frame above the middle top edge of each pane prevents accidental falling inwards of the glass when the tank is emptied.

COMPRESSED AIR

In the new aquarium compressed air is used for two purposes

only: (1) for lifting water from lower levels to the surface, thereby assisting water movement within the tanks; (2) for imparting a rippled surface to bring about a play of light and shade over rocks and gravel, as occurs naturally in shallower regions of the sea.

The air is bubbled up inside pipes (concealed behind two window mullions on the north side), or in tank corners behind polythene sheets (Figs 27 and 28). Water is drawn in through holes near the bottom of the pipes or sheets and gushes out through slits slightly above water level. Experience and experiment show that such 'air-pipe pumps' use compressed air much more effectively than diffusers sited openly on tank floors.

LIGHTING

It is hardly possible to light an aquarium satisfactorily with daylight. Daylight is too variable in intensity and whatever the orientation of the tanks some will always be more brightly lit than others. When the sun shines, strong reflections of the sunny side will be seen in the darker side unless a curtain is hung down the middle of the public hall. Too much daylight induces rapid growth of small algae, which on dying break up and produce silt; the result is dirty tanks. Back-lighting from windows behind the tanks, a standard feature of many Victorian public aquaria, some of which still survive, illuminates the sides of the fish away from the viewer and leaves the backs of the tanks in semi-darkness. A few translucent objects—some sea anemones, ascidians, dogfish-eggs, etc—look well when back-lit, but the majority of opaque animals do not. The tanks should be more strongly lit than the public hall, to avoid as far as possible having reflections of people in the glass, and to make the tanks appear as a series of bright living pictures within their darker frames.

Illumination of the tanks here is by a number of reflector-type bulbs such as Phillips Spot-floods, 100 watt, and Crompton 150 watt Spotlights. These are arranged so as to illuminate areas of the tanks, and being fitted in adjustable mountings can easily be swivelled. It has been found that sudden illumination of a tank, or the equally sudden switching-off of lights can cause considerable disturbance to some species; so an automatic dimming device has been incorporated into the circuit.

In addition to the main lights, low-wattage bulbs in water-proof plastic bulkhead fittings fixed at a small number of places on the ceiling directly above the tanks are switched on whenever the main lights are off. These night-lights give sufficient illumination for a number of active fishes to avoid obstructions at night. They probably help the mackerel and some other pelagic fish and they definitely do help smooth hounds (*Mustelus mustelus*) and spur dogs (*Squalus acanthias*) to avoid bumping their snouts on rocks in the dark. The provision of night-lights was recommended long ago by Saville Kent as a result of his experience in the former Manchester Aquarium (opened 1874), and their benefit to these same species was noticed independently at Plymouth some years ago.

ROCKWORK

Few fishes are completely at ease in a bare-walled tank. Many invertebrates and some fishes need to be provided with rocky nooks and crannies and with a floor of natural sands or gravels. When an aquarium is intended to attract a paying public, the appearance of this rockwork and the treatment of the tank walls is of paramount importance in providing an aesthetically pleasing background for the animals. The success or otherwise of the scenic presentation cannot fail to influence receipts at the cash desk.

As this particular aquarium is intended almost entirely for local marine life, it was decided to base the scenic presentation on local rocks, and of these the beautiful Devonian limestone forming the northern boundary of Plymouth Sound was considered most suitable. The rock is very hard and is often bluish-white in colour, pink or streaked with pink. Water-worn rocks of various sizes could be picked up from higher tidal levels, and by careful attention to bedding planes could be built into natural-looking cliffs in the tanks. In addition to the use of real rocks, rubber-latex moulds were made of small portions of

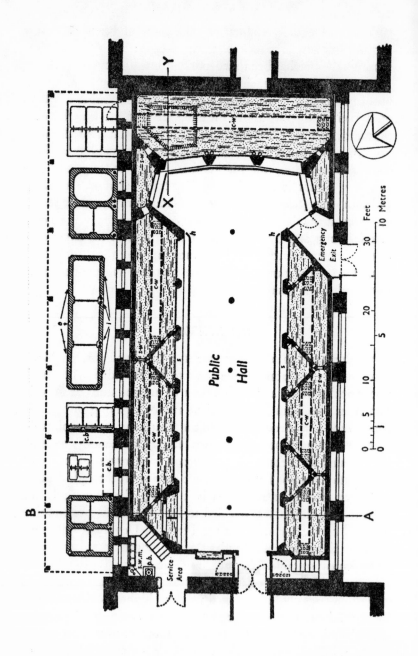

Public Hall

Service Area

Emergency Exit

Y

X

A

B

Feet
10 Metres

0   5   10   20   30

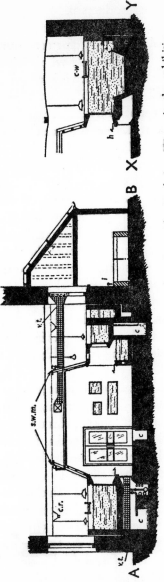

Fig 27 (facing page) Plan of aquarium at Plymouth and outside circulation. Water in the exhibition tanks is indicated by line and dot stippling. c, sea-water return culvert; c.b, circulation bench; c.r, over-flows; i, inflows; o, overflows; p.b, plunger head conveyor rail (Henderson track); c-w, cat-walk; h, hand-rail; i, inflows; o, overflows; p.b, plunger bucket; s, sill; s-w, swim-ways; s.w.m, sea-water main

Fig 28   Section of aquarium at Plymouth

water-worn cliff faces and used to produce artificial rock 'tiles'. One face of each tile exactly reproduces the shape and texture of the natural rock on which the mould was made. The other face, being flat and scored, forms a 'key' for cementing to the back walls, especially of the triangular tanks where it is necessary to keep the thickness of the added rockwork to a minimum. Joints between adjacent rock tiles are filled with cement and sand and modelled to merge the natural mouldings of the various tiles into one apparently solid rock face. A little of the rockwork in one triangular tank is seen in Figs 27 and 28.

A strong mix (1:3) of sulphate-resisting cement and crushed limestone which had passed a ¼in sieve was used in making tiles. Before filling the moulds with the mix, the rubber was wetted with a strong solution of Teepol to prevent the adhesion of air bubbles and, after filling, the moulds were vibrated to eliminate all air trapped in the mix. For fixing the tiles to the tank walls a stronger mix (1:2) of sulphate-resisting cement, fine sands and waterproofer was used. Finally, the artificial rock faces were painted to resemble natural rocks. The epoxy resin paints used are non-toxic, are very hard and should withstand repeated cleaning. The final effect is excellent, it being difficult to distinguish artificial rocks from natural and impossible once they are covered with natural growths.

Where the back wall of a tank is left bare it is painted with epoxy resin paint of a moderately dark-green shade to stimulate the effect of the greenness seen on looking through many feet of sea water. Near the backs of certain tanks, frosted (sandpapered) sheets of Perspex pleasantly diffuse the background to give an appearance of distance; they eliminate shadows which would otherwise show on the walls. Scenic paintings of apparently distant rocks on the walls behind such sheets increase this illusion of remote vistas. The sheets are mostly 6in in front of the back wall of the tank, but sometimes are further away and fish allowed to pass behind. They are held by slotted slates hidden in the rockwork. In arranging such sheets it is essential that side and bottom edges be concealed from view, for if seen the illusion is destroyed.

The angled-out side walls of the larger tanks are painted white, again with epoxy resins. This white surface is, of course, invisible to the public and it helps to reflect back into the tank some light which would otherwise be lost. To conceal the far corners of these tanks, with their inflows and swim-ways, rock cliffs are built against the side walls a little in front of them. Fish can pass out of sight behind these cliffs, but most fishes remain on view. Only lobsters, dogfishes, conger eels and wrasses have been troublesome, often hiding in the concealed corners, and special measures are taken to deal with them. Thus if there are more lobsters in a tank than there are hidden corners, some will be forced to occupy holes in full view. Fish swimming into view from behind these cliffs and disappearing again behind them seem to come and go as they would naturally do among rocks in the sea.

After the rockwork was built, the bottom of every tank was covered with a layer of sulphate-resisting cement and sand, to which a suitable yellow colouring agent had been added, and rendered to a thickness of 1in. While still wet the rendering was strewn with sand or gravel, gently patted in by hand and given a rippled surface as on a sandy seashore. Now, when fish disturb the loose sand or gravel, the rippling helps to retain it in position, and where patches of floors are uncovered they match well with the sand or gravel and do not look like bare concrete. It is important that the bottom screeding be carried out after the rockwork is in position so that rocks emerge from it as from a natural deposit.

The total quantity of sea water held by the reservoirs is about 110,000 gallons when both are completely full, while the total quantity of water in aquarium and service tanks is roughly 25,000 gallons. At the present time the water is circulated at a rate of about 5,000 gallons an hour. All sea water piping is ABS plastic, which employs a solvent/welding principle. All that has to be done is that one end of the joint is 'painted' with the solvent and joined with the other end, thus forming a simple and perfect joint.

All valves in the circulation system are Saunders-type, a

screw-down type which presses a rubber diaphragm on to a vulcathene or ABS saddle. In this way no metal comes into contact with the circulating sea water. (ABS piping is produced by Durapipe Ltd.)

16

THE SCHOOL MARINE AQUARIUM

The educational applications of a marine aquarium are both varied and extensive. From a biological point of view there is the exciting possibility of letting children observe a great variety of animal and plant life. At its simplest it can be used as a passing centre of interest. It can also be developed along certain lines for a more profound study of marine life.

Some teachers will want the children to collect their own specimens, and the aquarium may well become the end-point of some field work. In our work on the seashore we have noticed time and time again that a child working on animal populations of a particular seashore zone begins to ask questions about the molluscs. Many of these can be answered by keeping particular species and observing them. This work has the great advantage that no animals are killed, for they can all be returned to the same shore as soon as the work is completed. The teaching of sound conservation principles is vastly important at a time when great pressures are being applied to all coastal regions.

So often the soundest educational work can be done on broadly-based ideas and the fundamentals of energy cycles, food-pyramid of numbers, and food chains can all be learned from the school aquarium.

The movement of fishes can be observed by watching a few species such as butterfish, blennies, scorpionfish, flatfish and small eels. We have watched a blenny literally climb out on to a rock, and apart from the intense interest of such a happening the specialised use of fins was plainly demonstrated. Children will soon become fascinated by the rippling body movement of an eel, and will soon be able to compare this movement with the swimming action of a baby flatfish or the sudden darting of a scorpionfish. There are enough species on the shore to cover the gamut of movement and fin adaptation and to help the youngest child realise that all fish do not swim 'like goldfish'. The method of locomotion of starfish is plainly observed by letting them move along the front glass, when each tube foot can be seen in action. Shellfish carefully selected will demonstrate a further range of movement, and all the varied modifications to the foot that has led them to such success as individual species.

Necklace shells and netted dog-whelks bulldoze through the sand using their foot as a kind of bulldozer; limpets use their foot to cling to rocks and resist the powerful force of the waves; razorfish have a foot which is a most effective digging organ, and cockles somersault and roll and bury with the aid of their foot. Ragworms will swim if placed on the surface of the water and then burrow down on reaching the sand.

Again, the aquarium can frequently be used as a demonstration unit, and the species should then be returned to the shore when no longer required. However, a word of caution. Many sea animals are disturbed by transfer from shore to tank, and their behaviour on introduction often comprises a sudden burst for cover or a mad rushing to and fro in great panic. Once you know your species it is not difficult to pick the ones you need to demonstrate a particular point.

Feeding is one of the most stimulating experiences for children to watch. Younger ones in particular always want to know 'where the mouth is', and since many species do not possess a recognisable mouth, feeding time helps to provide a few answers. Nor should we assume that senior students are in any way familiar with the forms we can keep in the aquarium. In the rush towards their qualification examinations, field work, and the observation of living material too often become neglected. A biology course based on examination subjects can still be treated imaginatively and the young people offered the delight of dealing with living animals. Few of them may know that sea urchins have five teeth, which can be seen quite plainly if the urchin is persuaded to hold on to the glass with its tube feet whilst a portion of food is placed on its test. Most interesting of all is the commensal relationships of the hermit crab with its ragworm and sea anemone. Here we have three animals sharing their food and fortune in a mutually protective partnership. The hermit crab, being the active predator, secures the food; the ragworm takes its share from the crab's mouth, and when these have fed and moved on, the sea anemone bends over, and working somewhat like a vacuum cleaner clears up what is left.

In springtime and early summer the spawning activities of many species can be observed, and in this connection crustaceans and molluscs are particularly obliging. To see a stream of zoea larvae drifting free from a hermit crab is an unforgettable experience and perfectly indicative of the process of plankton 'birth' taking place on a much greater scale in the sea itself.

Experimental work is most difficult to undertake on the shore, but simple work of this kind can be developed within the confines of a tank. Much of it will arise directly from field work carried out on the shore.

Apart from the obvious biological applications, a well-displayed tank is aesthetically pleasing. As such it has an important place both in the decor of the school and inspirational work in the fields of art and sculpture. The unique shapes, varied colour and contrasting movements will lead the children to produce some delightful original work. Perhaps the hidden assets of a marine aquarium are most valuable in the classroom where children have a prodigious appetite for new experiences.

17

PHOTOGRAPHY IN THE AQUARIUM

The shapes, colours and behaviour of marine creatures make them perfect subjects for photography. The marine aquarist who has no experience of photographic work is ideally situated to start. Photographic equipment ranges, of course, from extremely sophisticated gear to quite simple and inexpensive pocket cameras, and the beginner is well advised to consider the purchase of good secondhand equipment. This is advertised in photographic magazines and is also on sale at local camera shops.

CHOICE OF CAMERA

The ideal camera is a single-lens reflex and the format can be 35mm, or 2¼in square, or 5 by 7in; 35mm has the advantage of bringing a very wide range of both cameras and accessories at reasonable prices, and film is fairly cheap.

Large formats are often more expensive but have the advantage that if you want to produce large enlargements above 10 by 12in the pictures will be sharper. For most purposes, however, you will probably not want a larger black and white print than 10 by 8in and for this a 35mm camera gives beautiful definition and sharpness. For most of us the cheaper ones do the job just as well as those super ones.

The reason for choosing a single-lens reflex camera is that you can focus exactly on the subject up to the moment of taking the picture, and you know that if it looks in focus it will give a sharp image on the negative. Since most of your work will be done within the confines of a small tank you will need to be able to focus as close as 16in. To get that close to your subject it will be necessary to have a detachable lens, and the single-lens reflex (SLR) has this, so that extension tubes can be inserted between the lens and the camera. A set of extension tubes consists of three different-sized tubes to give you a varied combination of magnifications when they are used in conjunction with the lens.

You can choose between non-automatic and automatic lenses; the latter are more expensive but well worth the extra cost. At the time of writing there are an increasing number of macro-lenses coming on to the market and many of these have a zoom action, focusing from 50mm which gives similar coverage to a standard lens, into a close-up which allows you to photograph the head of a prawn and have it fill the frame. The quality of these lenses is superb and they are thoroughly recommended for close-up photography in tanks.

So far then we recommend: *35mm single-lens reflex camera with a set of extension tubes or with a macro-lens.*

In order to keep the camera steady a tripod is essential. Take a look around your local photographic dealers and choose the one which suits both your requirements and pocket.

THE PHOTOGRAPHIC SET UP

In order to take pictures through the front glass of an aquarium tank, a few basic requirements must be understood.

1. The subject will need lighting from above and from the front.
2. Top light must be shielded so that it does not flash on to the front of the camera lens.
3. Front light must be at an angle of 45° to the front glass, or otherwise its light will reflect back into the camera.
4. The camera should ideally point slightly down or up or otherwise the lens will be reflected in your picture.
5. The face of the glass you intend to photograph through must be absolutely clean and free from any dirt or dust. Salt water leaves smears that can only be cleaned away with fresh water or a window-cleaning preparation.

Let's now take as an example preparations for a typical photo session. First we arrange a suitable background, and perhaps add a few rocks or other decoration to improve the picture. The tank must then be filtered or left to settle, because specks in the water come out as tiny white dots on your photograph and completely spoil the effect.

Then introduce your specimen—say a starfish.

Check that lighting is correct and take a reading with a meter. Set your lens and speed.

By using a plastic rod, 'persuade' the starfish into the required position, put the lights on, focus and take your picture.

To get a successful picture is nothing like as simple as the description makes it sound but with just a little perseverance you will soon be able to do so.

BACKGROUNDS

It is important to have the background as uncluttered as possible and for this reason do not use complicated sets of tangled seaweeds and barnacle-covered rocks. Sheets of coloured Perspex or plastic can be slid against the back glass either on the inside or outside and the colour varied to suit the subject. For colour photography it is the combination of *colours* that is important, but in black and white you need a contrasting *tone* to throw the subject into sharp relief. A less expensive background can be provided by sheets of coloured paper placed outside the glass, and even large areas of flat rocks can be placed well behind the back glass so as to be out of focus.

It is a definite advantage to keep the subject as close to the front of the glass as possible and this can be done by inserting a sheet of clear glass a short distance from the front. This helps to confine an active subject closer to the camera, and at the same time helps to throw the background out of focus by keeping the subject well away from it.

Whenever possible let the creature provide the colours, and allow your background to enhance them—not to conflict with them.

HABITAT SETS

If you wish your pictures to have added scientific value you should endeavour to include aspects of the natural habitat. Obvious examples are to provide sand for sandy-shore species or a rock for rocky-shore types. Care should be taken at such times to exclude any seaweed or other species not found in the zone inhabited by the animal you are photographing. The use of reference books will help sort these matters out for those not too conversant with the shore itself.

LIGHTING FOR TANK PHOTOGRAPHY

TUNGSTEN LIGHT. This form of lighting is created by household bulbs. It has a disadvantage in that, even if 150 watt bulbs are used, it is necessary to have some sort of lighting rig to hold the eight to ten bulbs you will need. These generate a good deal of heat which can soon increase the water temperature. However, the bulbs can be mounted in batten holders fixed to cross-pieces of wood fastened together and surrounded by some sort of screen to act as a shade. If the inside of this is covered with silver foil more light will be reflected down on to the subject. The whole rig should then be suspended above the tank so that the bulbs are at least 12in from the water surface.

Front lighting can be provided by using an adjustable lamp.

Tungsten light is not really suitable for colour film, and the serious photographer is advised to use either photofloods or electronic flash.

PHOTOFLOOD LIGHTING. These special photographic bulbs can be purchased from any good photographic supplier. They give an intense white light, but are also very hot when burning. Their life is shorter than household bulbs.

A variety of fittings are made to hold the bulbs, and quite inexpensive adjustable stands can be bought for front lighting.

ELECTRONIC FLASH. This is the ideal lighting system, due to its high-speed flash stopping movement, its lack of heat and its suitability for colour or black and white film. These facts, together with the intensity of illumination, make it the lighting used by all professionals.

The best buy is a unit with two synchronised flash-heads, both being fired by your pressing the camera release. One of these flash-heads should be hung over the tank and the other positioned to give front lighting.

Non-synchronised heads can be used, providing you buy a synchroniser. This is connected to one flash-head and is placed so as to receive light from the other flash which is fired by the camera.

A wide variety of electronic flash equipment is available, so study what is advertised in photographic journals.

REMEMBER. When using any form of electric lighting for tank photography you should ensure that there is no possibility of wire trailing into the water, nor any chance of the rigs falling into or coming into contact with water.

CINE FILMING

By their very nature animals of all kinds are ideal subjects for movies. The beginner may well be content with simple shots of fish swimming and crabs eating, but without doubt if he is an interested film maker he will soon want to get those big close-ups of action, so it is as well to think about choice of equipment right at the start.

CHOOSING YOUR MOVIE CAMERA. Whether you decide on Super 8, 16 or 35mm gauge is purely a matter of the depth of your pocket, but whichever gauge you decide upon the following points should be considered.

1. A reflex viewing system should be regarded as a basic minimum. With this system you can view the action through the lens, whilst filming and focusing is thus simplified.

2. It is useful to have a camera with a variety of lenses of detachable design. Built-in lenses severely limit the potential of any camera.

3. It is useful to have a system whereby a variety of filming speeds can be used, so that certain actions can be slowed down and others speeded up where necessary.

These three are most important, and after that you might like to consider a through-the-lens metering system and a battery operation for long running-on sequences.

Super 8 is ideal for home consumption but you will need 16mm gauge if you are going to try professional work. Television companies will not take anything less. 35mm gives superb quality but is simply too expensive to run for the amateur.

If you decide on a camera with detachable lenses, you may well find yourself considering a 16mm in any case, as few Super 8 cameras have this facility. For 16mm you could use a standard 25mm, a 75mm and perhaps a larger telephoto—or again perhaps a zoom which combines the focal lengths of many lenses.

Extension tubes are another useful item—when used in conjunction with a 25mm or 75mm lens they will enable you to get those exciting shots of a crab's eye or a close-up of eggs.

A good tripod is essential. It should be firm and light, and have a smooth action pan and tilt-head, with a good long handle for controlling camera movement. Some tripods are very heavy, and although this matters little when used in the home, it becomes a real problem if it has to be carried long distances in the field.

Two simple rules should be written large on every cine camera:

1. Always use a tripod.
2. Pan and tilt as little as possible. Don't move the camera more than necessary—always let the subject do the movement.

TECHNIQUES. These come mostly with practice, for they depend so much on the individual approach to film-making, and the set-up you have. To help you there is one book that is essential to the amateur film maker, *Making Wildlife Movies* by Christopher

Parsons. (NB available in USA—Stackpole, Harrisburg.) Chris Parsons is a television producer who has made wildlife films all over the world on every subject from ants to antelopes and from eels to elephants. Having made several films with him we co-operated on some sections of the book and marine filming features in it—described in much more detail than can be done here.

CHOICE OF FILM. At the present time there is little purpose in using black and white film, although it has the great advantage of considerably greater speed. Every cine enthusiast has his personal choice of film and often the choice will be dictated by whether the filming is in natural or artificial light.

But the beginner will do well to consider whether to use a reversal film or negative film. If the film is likely to have many projections, your choice is between a reversal film such as Ektachrome, or a negative-positive process such as Eastman-color. The one snag with a reversal type is that you only have one copy and once that gets scratched there's nothing you can do to restore it, whereas a negative type can be used to make a copy for projection, and then stored safely to be available for future copies, should you need them.

MAKING YOUR FILM. To make an interesting film to show to your friends means a great deal of thoughtful planning before, during and after the actual camera work.

To begin with you need a simple story line—it may be the life of a rock pool as seen through four seasons, or the life history of a blenny.

When filming do remember to vary your shots.

1. You need a variety of shot sizes.
2. You need frequent change of angle, combined with 1 above.
3. Try to get some unusual angles by shooting from above or very low down.

Later when you are editing the film, try to throw out every shot that is out of focus, badly lit, wobbly or just plain dull. Most of your shots will run too long, so cut them. There are, of course, times when you will want a sequence to run a while, for instance if it is showing interesting behaviour; but in general, short shots properly assembled lead to a snappy film that is much more interesting to watch.

Of one thing you can be certain, you will find endless pleasure and interest in filming or photographing underwater life. There will be times when the camera reveals facets of life you never realised existed. The eye of the camera will help you to see new wonders in your marine tank which, thoughtfully filmed, you can bring to your friends as well.

ACKNOWLEDGEMENTS

I have been particularly fortunate in being helped by a wealth of friends, but in particular, I acknowledge help given by the staff of the Marine Biological Association UK.

Then there are the fishermen like Herbie Bewley, Mike Cornish, Ken Browse, Terry Ekers, and Tom and Fred Jones, who through the years have brought in specimens and who have so unselfishly collected for me.

My aquarium partner, David Halfhide, helped make the idea of our aquarium into reality.

On the photographic side, especially in film making, I thank the BBC Natural History Unit, among whom producers Chris Parsons and Richard Brock, and cameraman George Shears, have given so much helpful advice over the years. Also to my filming partner Ron Peggs, who with me has spent countless hours on beaches here and abroad.

Lastly, there are all those eager young schoolchildren who have explored the shore with me, whose enthusiasm has always provided inspiration and whose endless questions have kept alive a spirit of enquiry.

FOR FURTHER REFERENCE

Books on marine life are innumerable and they range from highly technical and scientific publications to popular handbooks. The following list is by no means a full one, but contains books known to the author that are recommended for marine aquarists. Many of the books in this list are now out of print, but they are included because they can still be obtained from good second-hand bookshops or from libraries.

BARRETT, J. H. & YONGE, C. M. *Pocket Guide to the Seashore*, Collins, 1958

BRIGHTWELL, L. R. *Down to the Sea*, Isaac Pitman, 1954

DICKINSON, C. I. *British Seaweeds*, Eyre & Spottiswoode, 1963

EALES, N. B. *The Littoral Fauna of Great Britain*, Cambridge, 1939

GOSSE, Philip Henry. Writer of many Victorian books on the seashore and the aquarium. Secondhand copies occasionally available in bookshops

HAAS, W. de & KNORR, F. *Marine Life*, Burke, 1966

HARDY, Alister. *The Open Sea. The World of Plankton*, New Naturalist Series, Collins, 1956

JACKMAN, Leslie, A. J. *Exploring the Seashore*, Evans, 1970

——. *The Beach*, Evans, 1974

——. *The Marine Aquarium in School*, Teachers' Leaflets, Warne, 1956

JENKINS, Travis. *The Fishes of the British Isles*, Frederick Warne, 1925

JOHNSON, J., SCOTT, A. & CHADWICK, H. C. *Marine Plankton*, Liverpool University Press, 1924

KENNEDY, Michael. *The Sea Angler's Fishes*, Hutchinson, 1954

LYTHGOE, John & Gillian. *Fishes of the Seas*, Blandford Press, 1971

McMILLAN, Nora F. *British Shells*, Frederick Warne, 1968

PARSONS, Christopher. *Making Wildlife Movies*, David & Charles

Marine Biological Association UK. *Plymouth Marine Fauna*, 3rd ed, 1957

RUSSELL, F. S. & YONGE, C. M. *The Seas*, Frederick Warne, 1928

SPOTTE, Stephen H. *Fish and Invertebrate Culture. Water Management in Closed Systems*, Wiley—Interscience New York, 1970

STRATTON, L. W. *Your Book of Shell Collecting*, Faber & Faber, 1968

STEP, E. *Shell Life*, Frederick Warne, 1901

STEPHENSON, T. A. *British Sea Anemones*, vols I to II, The Ray Society

STREET, P. *Between the Tides*, University of London Press, 1963

TEBBLE, N. *British Bivalve Seashells*, British Museum, 1966

VEVERS, H. G. *The British Seashore*, Routledge & Kegan Paul, 1954

WACHTEL, Hellmuth. *Aquarium Hygiene*, Studio Vista, 1966

WILSON, D. P. *Life of the Shore and Shallow Sea*, Ivor Nicholson & Watson, 1935

——. *They Live in the Sea*, Collins, 1947

YONGE, C. M. *The Sea Shore*, Collins, 1949

INDEX